THE POWER
OF INTEGRITY

THE
POWER
of
INTEGRITY

*Building a Life
Without Compromise*

JOHN F. MACARTHUR, JR.

CROSSWAY BOOKS • WHEATON, ILLINOIS
A DIVISION OF GOOD NEWS PUBLISHERS

The Power of Integrity

Copyright © 1997 by John F. MacArthur, Jr.

Published by Crossway Books
      a division of Good News Publishers
      1300 Crescent Street
      Wheaton, Illinois 60187

Cover design: D² DesignWorks

First printing, 1997

Printed in the United States of America

Unless otherwise indicated, Bible quotations are taken from the *New American Standard Bible*, copyright © 1960, 1962, 1963, 1968, 1971, 1972, 1973, 1977 by the Lockman Foundation and used by permission.

Library of Congress Cataloging-in-Publication Data
MacArthur, John, 1939-
    The power of integrity : building a life without compromise / John
F. MacArthur, Jr.
        p.   cm.
    Includes index.
    ISBN 0-89107-942-4
    1. Integrity—Religious aspects—Christianity.   I. Title.
BV4647.I55M33   1997
241'.4—dc21   97-7861

05		04		03		02		01		00		99		98		97
15	14	13	12	11	10	9	8	7	6	5	4	3	2	1

CONTENTS

INTRODUCTION

We live in a world of compromise—in a society that has abandoned moral standards and Christian principles in favor of expediency or pragmatism. The underlying philosophy is based on accomplishing goals by whatever means are necessary. This self-centered perspective should have as its motto: "If it works for you, do it"—a notion that inevitably leads to compromise of conscience and convictions. Because compromise is so prevalent in our society, you could say we no longer have a national conscience; guilt and remorse are nonfactors in determining behavior.

Politicians, who should be upholding the high ideals of our country, instead are leading the way in compromise. They promote their lofty standards and high ideals prior to their elections but compromise them once they are in office. The same holds true in business, from corporate executives down to salespeople; in the courts, from judges to attorneys; in sports, from owners to athletes; and in all walks of life. As a result, people learn to lie, cheat, steal, and shade the truth—to do whatever is necessary to get what they want. Thus compromise becomes a way of life.

Unfortunately, the philosophy and practice of compromise has even invaded the church. Because tolerance is the operative ideology in our society, the church adopts a similar perspective to reach the unsaved. Many churches now look for ways to give the Gospel to people without offending them. Yet the very nature of the Gospel is offensive because it confronts sinners with their sin. Ignoring that, many churches willingly compromise God's Word instead of standing firm on the Gospel, and they give the world a watered-down version that can't effect any change.

On an individual basis, the spirit of compromise hits closer to home in your personal interactions. You may have had opportunities to proclaim Christ to unbelievers, yet out of intimidation or lack of confidence, you have kept silent. Perhaps you've found yourself compromising God's Word on some ethical issue at work or in your neighborhood and convinced yourself that such compromise was necessary to maintain your credibility as an employee or neighbor. Yet your Christian testimony is predicated on your complete devotion to God's Word as the highest authority—no matter what the consequences may be. God draws the elect into the kingdom through Christians who prove to be different from the world—who reveal their true allegiance by their commitment and obedience to God's standards.

Our difficulty in living like that is the opposition we encounter from the world. R.C. Sproul, in his book *Pleasing God*, describes the pull the world has on us:

> The world is a seducer. It seeks to attract our attention and our devotion. It remains so close at hand, so visible, so enticing. It eclipses our view of heaven. What is seen vies for our attention. It entices our eyes lest we look up for a better country whose builder and maker is God. It pleases us—much of the time, anyway—and, alas, we often live our lives to please it. And that is where conflict ensues, for pleasing the world so seldom overlaps with pleasing God.
>
> The divine call we receive is this: "Do not be conformed to this world" (Rom. 12:2). But the world wants us to be partners with it. We are urged to participate in the fullness of it. It presses upon us with the ultimate peer pressure. ([Wheaton, Ill.: Tyndale House, 1988], 59)

The church is now so adept at compromising with the world that it has forgotten how to be uncompromising. That's because we readily accept the world's value systems and indulge ourselves in them to the point that we personalize them and they become our desires. In essence our standards replace God's.

Scripture calls us to the opposite of compromise. From one end of the Bible to the other, God clearly commands his people to live apart from the world.

When God established the nation Israel, He built into the Israelites' daily living the principle of separation from the world. Their religious observances throughout the year served as safeguards to prevent them, as a unique people (Deut. 14:2), from intermingling with pagans.

Likewise, God calls all His people to be separate from the world (1 Pet. 2:9). Whenever we are tempted to compromise, we need only remind ourselves that God never compromises His absolute truths and principles for expediency. He always lives according to His Word. Psalm 138:2 says, "Thou hast magnified Thy word according to all Thy name." God is committed to His Word, and as His children, we are to be also.

When you view God's Word as the ultimate authority, that opens the way for developing integrity instead of compromise. *The American Heritage Dictionary* (Houghton Mifflin, 1992) defines integrity as "steadfast adherence to a strict moral or ethical code," "the state of being unimpaired; soundness," or "the quality or condition of being whole or undivided; completeness." It comes from the word *integer*, which means "whole" or "complete." Integrity essentially means being true to one's ethical standards, in our case, God's standards. Its synonyms are honesty, sincerity, incorruptibility. It describes someone without hypocrisy or duplicity—someone who is completely consistent with his or her stated convictions. A person who lacks integrity—someone who says one thing and does another—is a hypocrite.

Nowhere is integrity more critical than in the leadership of the church, because the spiritual leader must maintain integrity to set a credible example for all to follow. Yet there are many in leadership who lack integrity and thus by definition are hypocrites.

Our Lord has no patience for such people. The scribes and Pharisees were frequent subjects of Christ's blistering attacks on their hypocrisy. Of them He said, "They say things, and do not do them" (Matt. 23:3). That is a lack of integrity—they lived by one set of ethics while commanding others to live by another. After pronouncing several woes on them, Jesus offered this final rebuke: "You serpents, you brood of vipers, how shall you escape the sentence of hell?" (v. 33).

But to the man of integrity, God promises blessing. When Solomon finished building the house of the Lord, the Lord appeared to him and said:

> *"I have heard your prayer and your supplication, which you have made before Me; I have consecrated this house which you have built by putting My name there forever, and My eyes and My heart will be there perpetually. And as for you, if you will walk before Me as your father David walked, in integrity of heart and uprightness, doing according to all that I have commanded you and will keep My statutes and My ordinances, then I will establish the throne of your kingdom over Israel forever, just as I promised to your father David, saying, 'You shall not lack a man on the throne of Israel.'"*
>
> —1 Kings 9:3-5

The conclusion is simple: those who maintain a life of integrity will be blessed by God; those who don't will be cursed, especially those in spiritual leadership.

Integrity is essential if any believer is to represent God and Christ in this world. Anything less than total devotion to our Lord in both character and conduct amounts to compromise with the world. A mistake often made by well-meaning Christians is to go too far in the other direction—to adhere to the biblical code of conduct without the proper internal motivation. That, too, is hypocrisy.

How to cultivate integrity from righteous motives is the scope of this book.

The first part will examine the essentials to developing that motivation. That involves a desire to know Christ intimately, a commitment to the Word of God as the ultimate authority, and a desire to live a godly life. We will examine each of those in the first three chapters.

In the second section we'll look at some biblical examples of godly men who saw their integrity constantly tested. The book of Daniel will provide Old Testament examples of how Daniel and his three friends responded without compromise when tempted by worldly men to deny God. Our New Testament example will come from the apostle Paul. Throughout his ministry he endured attacks on his character, and in 2 Corinthians he answers those attacks and presents a model life of integrity.

The final section will show how you can manifest a life of integrity. Since the avoidance of hypocrisy is so critical, in the first chapter of this section we'll look at how disciplined effort on your part, coupled with complete dependence on God, is the key to conquering the temptation toward hypocritical living. The final three chapters will detail how you can actively cultivate integrity by examining your responsibilities and duties toward God, toward yourself, and toward others—both believers and unbelievers.

Ultimately this book's goal is that you will be able to answer the following questions as David did: "O Lord, who may abide in Thy tent? Who may dwell on Thy holy hill? He who walks with integrity, and works righteousness, and speaks truth in his heart" (Ps. 15:1-2).

—

THE ESSENTIALS OF INTEGRITY

—

CHAPTER

ONE

VALUE
UNSURPASSED

The uncompromising spirit of Olympic sprinter and Scotsman Eric Liddell was made famous by the award-winning film *Chariots of Fire*. For months Liddell trained to run the 100-meter dash at the Paris Olympics in 1924. Sportswriters across Britain predicted he would win. But when the schedules were announced, Liddell discovered that the heats for his race were to be run on a Sunday. Because he believed he would dishonor God by competing on the Lord's Day, he refused to enter the race.

Eric's fans were stunned. Some who previously praised him called him a fool. But he stood firm. Professor Neil Campbell, a fellow student-athlete at the time, describes Liddell's decision:

> Liddell was the last person to make a song and dance about that sort of thing. He just said, "I'm not running on a Sunday"—and that was that. And he would have been very upset if anything much had been made of it at the time. We thought it was completely in character, and a lot of the athletes were quietly impressed by it. They felt that here was a man who was prepared to stand for what he thought was right, without interfering with anyone else, and without being dogmatic. (Sally Magnuson, *The Flying Scotsman* [New York: Quartet, 1981], 40)

Unlike the film version, which takes dramatic license with the facts, Liddell knew about the heat schedule months before the

Olympics. He also declined to run in the 4 x 100 and 4 x 400 meter relays, races that he had qualified for, because their heats also were to be run on Sunday. Since he was such a popular athlete, the British Olympic Committee asked if he would train to run in the 400 meters—a race he had performed well in before, but one he'd never considered seriously. He decided to train for it and discovered that he was a natural at that distance. His wife, Florence, says of his decision, "Eric always said that the great thing for him was that when he stood by his principles and refused to run in the 100 metres, he found that the 400 metres was really his race. He would not of known that otherwise" (Magnuson, 45).

Liddell went on to win the 400 meters and set a world record in the process. God honored his uncompromising spirit. But what was there about Eric Liddell that gave him the resolve to stand firm with his decision in spite of the pressure from the authorities and the press? The filmmakers of *Chariots of Fire* unknowingly provide the answer in a scene dramatizing the British Olympic authorities' attempt to change Liddell's mind about running in the 100 meters. After their unsuccessful attempt, one of the men comments, "The lad . . . is a true man of principle and a true athlete. His speed is a mere extension of his life—its force. We sought to sever his running from himself." In spite of the writer's labeling God as a generic "force," the statement is true. The Christian life cannot be lived apart from God. To do so is to compromise your very being.

That's where the power of integrity begins. Only as you and I derive our being from our relationship with Christ can we ever hope to live like He did, to suffer like He did, to withstand adversity like He did, and to die like He did—all without compromising.

The heart and soul of all Christianity is our relationship with Christ. Our salvation begins with Him, our sanctification progresses with Him, and our glorification ends with Him. He is the reason for our being, and thus He is more valuable to us than anyone or anything.

The apostle Paul knew well that the heart of the Christian life is building an intimate knowledge of Christ. That's why he said, "I count all things to be loss in view of the surpassing value of knowing Christ Jesus my Lord" (Phil. 3:8). That was both his passion and his "goal" (v. 14).

What were the "all things" he considered as loss? They were the ultimate credentials of the works-righteousness religion Paul served before coming to know Christ. He was "circumcised the eighth day, of the nation of Israel, of the tribe of Benjamin, a Hebrew of Hebrews; as to the Law, a Pharisee; as to zeal, a persecutor of the church; as to the righteousness which is in the Law, found blameless" (vv. 5-6). According to the conventional religious wisdom of his day, Paul followed the right rituals, was a member of the right race and tribe, adhered to the right traditions, served the right religion with just the right amount of intensity, and conformed to the right law with self-righteous zeal.

But one day when he was traveling to persecute more Christians, Paul met Jesus Christ (Acts 9). Paul saw Christ in all His glory and majesty, and he realized that all he thought was of value was worthless. So he says, "Whatever things were gain to me, those things I have counted as loss for the sake of Christ . . . and count them but rubbish in order that I may gain Christ" (v. 7-8). In Paul's mind, his assets had become liabilities—to such a degree that he considered them trash. Why? Because they couldn't produce what he thought they could—they couldn't produce righteousness, power, or endurance. And they couldn't lead him to eternal life and glory. So Paul gave up all His religious treasure for the treasure of knowing Christ deeply and intimately.

That is the essence of salvation—an exchange of something worthless for something valuable. Jesus illustrated the exchange in this way: "The kingdom of heaven is like a treasure hidden in the field, which a man found and hid; and from joy over it he goes and sells all that he has, and buys that field. Again, the kingdom of heaven is like a merchant seeking fine pearls, and upon finding one pearl of great value, he went and sold all that he had, and bought it" (Matt. 13:44-46). Those two men found something of far greater value than anything they owned. For them the decision was easy: sell all they thought was valuable for what was truly valuable.

That's what happens to those God chooses to bring into His kingdom. The person who comes to God is willing to pay whatever He requires, no matter how high the price. When confronted with his sin in the light of the glory of Christ—when God takes the blinders off his eyes—the repentant sinner suddenly realizes that nothing he held dear is worth keeping if it means losing Christ.

Jesus Christ is our treasure and our pearl. At some point in our lives we discovered that He was far more valuable than anything we had—whether possessions, fame, or desires. They all became valueless in comparison to Christ. So we trashed it all and turned to Him as our Savior and Lord. He became the supreme object of our affections. Our new desire was to know Him, love Him, serve Him, obey Him, and be like Him.

Is that still true of you? Is there anything in your life that competes with Christ? Is there anything in this world that captures your allegiance, devotion, and love more than Him? Do you still desire to know Him as much as you did when He first saved you? If not, you have compromised your relationship with Him and are dallying with the trash of the world. That is the danger of compromise.

If you are not careful to preserve and protect the treasure that is your relationship with Christ, the exuberance and devotion of your first days with Jesus can slowly and subtly turn into complacency and indifference. Eventually cold orthodoxy replaces loving obedience, and the result is a hypocritical life that will compromise with sin.

Fortunately for our sake, God has given us the resources in His Word to combat our tendency to sin and to restore our relationship with Christ. The apostle Paul shows us how by helping us see what we gained when we exchanged the trash for Christ. We have the benefits of a new life and a new relationship.

A NEW LIFE

When you were brought into God's kingdom, you were totally transformed. You became "a new creature; the old things passed away; behold, new things have come" (2 Cor. 5:17). You didn't just *receive* something new—you *became* someone new. Paul said, "I have been crucified with Christ, and it is no longer I who live, but Christ lives in me; and the life which I now live in the flesh I live by faith in the Son of God, who loved me, and delivered Himself up for me" (Gal. 2:20).

This new nature is not added to the old nature but replaces it— an exchange occurs. The transformed person is completely new. In contrast to the former love of evil, the new self—the deepest, truest part of a Christian—now loves the law of God, longs to fulfill its righteous demands, hates sin, and longs for deliverance from the unredeemed flesh—where sin still resides. Sin no longer controls you as it once did, but it still entices you to obey it instead of the Lord.

Knowing full well the temptation that sin is, Paul addressed the Ephesian Christians regarding their new nature. By contrasting the lifestyle of the wicked unbeliever with that of the spiritual Christian, he sought to demonstrate that a changed nature demands changed behavior. In 4:17-19 Paul describes the former wicked lifestyle we all followed: "Walk no longer as the Gentiles also walk, in the futility of their mind, being darkened in their understanding, excluded from the life of God, because of the igno-rance that is in them, because of the hardness of their heart; and they, having become callous, have given themselves over to sensu-ality, for the practice of every kind of impurity with greediness." The word "Gentiles" represents all ungodly, unregenerate, pagan people. Like the church in our day, the churches at Ephesus and in almost every non-Palestinian area in New Testament times were surrounded by rank paganism and its attendant immorality.

Centered on Christ

To believers who had fallen back into such degradation Paul writes, "But you did not learn Christ in this way" (Eph. 4:20). The phrase "learn Christ" is a direct reference to salvation. Anyone who makes a profession of faith in Christ ought to have nothing to do with the ways of the world, either by participation or association. James 4:4 says, "Friendship with the world is hostility toward God"; the ways of God and the ways of the world are not compatible. Any participation with the world is in effect a compromise of your new life.The very purpose of receiving Christ is to "be saved from this perverse generation" (Acts 2:40), and no one is saved who does not repent and forsake sin. To hold on to sin is to refuse God, to scorn His grace, and to nullify faith.

One of the first things we have to learn as Christians is not to trust our own thinking or rely on our own instincts. We now have the mind of Christ (1 Cor. 2:16), and His is the only mind we can rely on. When we are faithful and obedient to our Lord, we will think like Him, act like Him, love like Him, and in every possible way behave like Him, so that "whether we are awake or asleep, we may live together with Him" (1 Thess. 5:10).

To demonstrate the transforming nature of regeneration, Paul describes and defines the inherent realities of our new life in Christ. These are not exhortations—they are reminders of what occurred at the moment of conversion.

Strip Off the Old Self

Paul writes, "In reference to your former manner of life, you lay aside the old self, which is being corrupted in accordance with the lusts of deceit" (Eph. 4:22). In contrast to the unregenerate person who continually resists and rejects God, the Christian hears the call to "lay aside the old self." The verb means "to strip off," as you would take off dirty clothes. The tense indicates that this is a once-and-forever action that occurs at salvation.

The "old self" refers to believers in their unconverted state, which Paul describes as "being corrupted in accordance with the lusts of deceit." The gospel invitation is to lay aside that old self in repentance from sin, which includes not just sorrow about sin but a turning from sin to God.

Put On the New Self

As we lay aside the old self, we exchange it for something new: "Be renewed in the spirit of your mind, and put on the new self, which in the likeness of God has been created in righteousness and holiness of the truth" (Eph. 4:23-24). Colossians 3 and Romans 6 characterize this exchange as a union with Jesus Christ in His death and resurrection, which can also be described as the death of the "old self" and the resurrection of the "new self," who now walks in "newness of life." Our union with Christ and our new identity clearly demonstrate that salvation is transformation.

Our salvation also means we will think differently: "be renewed in the spirit of your mind." The best rendering of this present passive infinitive is as a modifier of the main verb "put on." That means the renewal of our minds is the consequence of laying aside the old self and is the context for putting on the new self.

When you became a Christian, God initially renewed your mind and gave you a completely new spiritual and moral capability. That renewal continues throughout your life as you obey God's will and His Word (cf. Rom. 12:1-2). This process is not a one-time accomplishment but a continual work of God's Spirit in you (Titus 3:5). Your resources in this process are always God's Word and prayer. Through them you gain the mind of Christ (Col. 3:16).

Your new self has been made in "the likeness of God [and] has been created in righteousness and holiness of the truth" (Eph. 4:24). That which was once darkened is now enlightened, learned in the truth, sensitive to sin, pure, and generous. Once characterized by wickedness and sin, we are now characterized by "righteousness and holiness." According to Peter, we are "partakers of the divine nature" (2 Pet. 1:4). Each of us now has a new self—a holy and righteous inner person fit for the presence of God. This is the believer's truest self.

To compromise this new self—this new creation—is the greatest injustice we can do to God. He saved us, transformed us, gave us a new nature, and renewed our minds. Thus the capacity to live a life of integrity is inherent in our new nature. You must grasp this fundamental element of your salvation before you can ever hope to build a life without compromise.

A NEW RELATIONSHIP

There is another aspect of your salvation that is just as vital: your new relationship with Jesus Christ. It is the one relationship you are to value above all others for two important reasons: the intimate communion possible with your Lord and Savior, and the wondrous benefits that union can bring.

Intimate Communion

As we discussed earlier in the chapter, the most valuable pursuit of Paul's life was "knowing Christ Jesus" (Phil. 3:8). To know Christ is not simply to have intellectual knowledge about Him; Paul uses the Greek verb *ginōskō*, which means to know "experientially" or "personally."

Paul taught the Ephesians that one of the functions of the church is to build up the people in "the knowledge of the Son of God" (4:13). There the word "knowledge" is from *epignōsis*, which refers to full knowledge that is correct and accurate. That is the knowing of which Jesus spoke when He said, "My sheep hear My voice, and I know them" (John 10:27). He was not speaking of merely knowing their identities but of knowing them intimately, and that is the way He wants His people to know Him. Paul's desire is for every believer to develop this deep knowledge of Christ by building a relationship with Him through prayer and faithful study of and obedience to God's Word.

Commentator F.B. Meyer describes our relationship with Christ in this way:

We may know Him personally, intimately, face to face. Christ does not live back in the centuries, nor amid the clouds of heaven: He is near us, with us, compassing our path and our lying down, and acquainted with all our ways. But we cannot know Him in this mortal life except through the illumination and teaching of the Holy Spirit . . . and we must surely know Christ, not as a stranger who turns in to visit for the night, or as the exalted King of men,—there must be the inner knowledge as of those whom He counts His own familiar friends, whom He trusts with His secrets, who eat with Him of His bread (Psalm xli. 9).

To know Christ in the storm of battle; to know Him in the valley of shadow; to know Him when the solar light irradiates our faces, or when they are darkened with disappointment and sorrow; to know the sweetness of His dealing with bruised reeds and smoking flax; to know the tenderness of His sympathy and the strength of His right hand—all this involves many varieties of experience on our part, but each of them, like the facets of a diamond, will reflect the prismatic beauty of His glory from a new angle. (*The Epistle to the Philippians* [Grand Rapids, Mich.: Baker, 1952, 162-63])

That's what it means to know Christ intimately. Growing in this deeper knowledge of Christ is a lifelong process that will not be complete until we see our Lord face to face.

A Beneficial Union

In addition to the personal interaction we have with Christ, several benefits accrue to those who have trusted in Him for salvation.

THE RIGHTEOUSNESS OF CHRIST.   Paul desired to "be.found in Him, not having a righteousness of my own derived from the Law, but that which is through faith in Christ, the righteousness which comes from God on the basis of faith" (Phil. 3:9). To know Christ is to have His righteousness, His holiness, and His virtue imputed to us, which makes us right before God.

Throughout his earlier life Paul tried to attain salvation

through strict adherence to the Law. But when he was confronted by the wondrous reality of Christ, he was ready to trade in all his self-righteous, external morals, good works, and religious rituals for the righteousness granted to him through faith in Jesus Christ. Paul was willing to lose the thin and fading robe of his reputation if he could only gain the splendid and incorruptible robe of the righteousness of Christ. This is the greatest of all benefits because it secures our standing before God. It is God's gift to the sinner, appropriated by faith in the perfect work of Christ, which satisfies God's justice.

THE POWER OF CHRIST. While having Christ's righteousness frees us from the penalty of sin, we are still subject to the control of sin. Fortunately, we have the power of Christ available to us to vanquish sin daily. If there is any doubt that His might is strong enough, Paul says it is "the power of His resurrection" (Phil. 3:10).

Christ's resurrection most graphically demonstrated the extent of His power. Raising Himself from the dead displayed His authority and control over both the physical world and the spiritual world. That's the kind of power Paul wanted to experience because he realized he was helpless to overcome sin on his own. His self-righteousness gained him nothing but the awareness of his inability to deal with sin.

The resurrection power of Christ deals with sin in two ways. First, as we discussed earlier, we experience His resurrection might at salvation. We were buried with Christ in His death, and we rose with Him to "walk in newness of life" (Rom. 6:4). But to defeat sin daily, we need His resurrection power to be our resource. We need His strength to serve Him faithfully, to conquer temptation, to overcome trials, and to witness boldly. We want to experience the potency of Christ to this degree: He "is able to do exceeding abundantly beyond all that we ask or think, according to the power that works within us" (Eph. 3:20). Only as we build our relationship with Christ and tap into His might will we have victory over sin in this life. And that is the only way we can build a life of integrity.

FELLOWSHIP WITH CHRIST. While Christ's power is our resource in our ongoing battle with sin, we have another problem: the suffering that is an unavoidable part of life. Because we live in a world full of pain and suffering, each one of us will experience suffering to one degree or another. The question is: Where can we turn when we need comfort? Paul says the answer is in our relationship with Christ because we can experience "the fellowship of His sufferings, being conformed to His death" (Phil. 3:10).

When we suffer, Christ is with us to comfort us during our heartache. Paul told the Corinthians, "Just as the sufferings of Christ are ours in abundance, so also our comfort is abundant through Christ" (2 Cor. 1:5). The degree to which He has already experienced the same suffering, and even more, is the reason He is able to comfort us. He was rejected by His own people, despised by the religious leaders, mocked by Roman soldiers, and crucified by all three. Yet He endured it all without sinning. He never once compromised God's law or God's plan of salvation in an attempt to ease His suffering.

The true test of your character is your response to the severest times of suffering and persecution. When suffering becomes too intense, the easy thing is to get angry and blame God. When persecution becomes too severe, the easy thing is to compromise your faith. To respond in either manner will cause you to miss out on the richest fellowship available to you. That's because the deepest moments of spiritual fellowship with the living Christ are the direct result of intense suffering. Suffering always drives us to Christ because we find in Him our merciful high priest who sympathizes "with our weaknesses" (Heb. 4:15) and who "was tempted in that which He has suffered, [and] is able to come to the aid of those who are tempted" (2:18). You need to view your sufferings as opportunities to be blessed by Christ as you find comfort in His fellowship.

THE GLORY OF CHRIST. The last benefit of this new relationship with Christ is a future one. Paul hopes to "attain to the resurrection from the dead" (Phil. 3:11). That is Paul's reference to the Rapture of the church, the day when Christ will return for His people and we will be transformed and will ultimately experience our freedom from the presence of sin. We long for that day because "our citizenship is in heaven, from which also we eagerly wait for a Savior, the Lord Jesus Christ; who will transform the body of our humble state into conformity with the body of His glory" (vv. 20-21).

That is the event for which each of us longs. On that day we will realize the completion of our salvation. Until then, we live in this world with the particular knowledge that our home is in heaven. That helps us live in the present because "every one who has this hope fixed on Him purifies himself, just as He is pure" (1 John 3:3). The best way to maintain integrity and avoid compromise is to keep your eyes focused on Christ. Allow Him free access to rule and guide your way through the world's toughest storms.

DOCTRINAL INTEGRITY

The old saying goes, "Every man has his price." Is that true? Do all of us have moral standards that are valid so long as they accommodate our personal goals and desires? Or are we willing to set aside our desires for the sake of those standards we claim to believe?

Church history is full of people who refused to compromise the biblical standards. As he stood before the Diet of Worms and was ordered to recant his writings or lose his life, Martin Luther did not deny Christ. Hugh Latimer and Nicholas Ridley, two English Reformers, were both burned at the stake for their faith in Christ. Those men are representative of the people who can't be bought; no price will cause them to sell out.

THE PRICE OF COMPROMISE

Men who hold to an uncompromising standard are sorely lacking in the church today. Many so-called Christians boast of their moral standards and extol their righteous character, yet abandon their conviction when compromise is more beneficial and expedient. Perhaps you recognize one or more of the following:

- People say they believe the Bible, yet attend churches where the Bible isn't taught.

- People agree that sin must be punished, but not if those sins are committed by their children.

- People oppose dishonesty and corruption until they must confront their bosses and risk losing their jobs.

- People maintain high moral standards until their lusts are kindled by unscriptural relationships.

- People are honest until a little dishonesty will save them money.

- People hold a conviction until it is challenged by someone they admire or fear.

Sadly, such compromises are not exceptions; they have become the rule. But don't think twentieth-century Christians are the only experts in the art of compromise. Scripture is full of people who compromised, including some very choice servants of God.

- Adam compromised God's law, followed his wife's sin, and lost paradise (Gen. 3:6, 22-24).

- Abraham compromised the truth, lied about Sarah's relationship to him, and nearly lost his wife (Gen. 12:10-12).

- Sarah compromised God's Word and sent Abraham to Hagar, who bore Ishmael and destroyed peace in the Middle East (Gen. 16:1-4, 11-12).

- Moses compromised God's command and lost the privilege of entering the Promised Land (Num. 20:7-12).

- Samson compromised his devotion as a Nazirite and lost his strength, his eyesight, and his life (Judg. 16:4-6, 16-31).

- Israel compromised the commands of the Lord, lived in sin, and, when fighting the Philistines, lost the Ark of God (1 Sam. 4:11). She also compromised the law of God with sin and idolatry and lost her homeland (2 Chron. 36:14-17).

- Saul compromised God's divine word by not slaying the animals of his enemy and lost his kingdom (1 Sam. 15:3, 20-28).

- David compromised God's standard, committed adultery with Bathsheba, murdered Uriah, and lost his infant son (2 Sam. 11:1—12:23).

- Solomon compromised his convictions, married foreign wives, and lost the united kingdom (1 Kings 11:1-8).

- Judas compromised his supposed devotion for Christ for thirty pieces of silver and was separated from Christ eternally (Matt. 26:20-25, 47-49; 27:1-5; cf. John 17:12).

- Peter compromised his conviction about Christ, denied Him, and lost his joy (Mark 14:66-72). Later he compromised the truth in order to gain acceptance by the Judaizers and lost his liberty (Gal. 2:11-14).

- Ananias and Sapphira compromised their word about their giving, lied to the Holy Spirit, and lost their lives (Acts 5:1-11).

Two observations come to mind from those examples. First, in every case the effect of the compromise was to lose something valuable in exchange for something temporary and unfulfilling, some sinful desire. How contrary that is to what we discovered in the first chapter. There we learned that you gain something valuable (your salvation and relationship with Christ) in exchange for something worthless (your sin and self-righteousness).

Second, note what was compromised in each of those examples: either God's Word, a command from God, or a conviction about God. Thus the true price of compromise is a rejection of God's Word, which amounts to rebellion against Him and promotion of self as the final authority.

That is the situation in many churches today. Even in churches that once were genuinely evangelical, where the Bible was the divine standard for belief and living, God's Word is now compromised. Sometimes it is stripped of its clear meaning or is relegated to a place of secondary authority. In many churches that once preached sound doctrine, evils that God plainly and repeatedly condemns are touted as acceptable. Scripture is often reinterpreted to accommodate those anti-biblical views. Pragmatism is in; commitment to biblical truth is denigrated as poor marketing strategy.

The fact is, people are content with unbiblical notions that raise their comfort level and either justify or overlook their sins. They are quick to reject as unloving anyone who presumes to hold them accountable to doctrinal beliefs and moral standards they deem outmoded and irrelevant.

Today the church is full of spiritual babies who are "tossed here and there by waves, and carried about by every wind of doctrine, by the trickery of men, by craftiness in deceitful scheming" (Eph. 4:14)—the antithesis of a spiritually mature Christian. Spiritual babies are in constant danger of falling prey to every new religious fad that comes along. Because they are not anchored in God's truth, they are subject to every sort of counterfeit truth—humanistic, cultic, pagan, demonic, or whatever. Just as families today are dominated by their children, so are many churches. How tragic when the church's immature believers are among its most influential teachers and leaders.

PROTECTING THE TRUTH

Where does the problem lie? Without question the fault lies primarily in the leadership—both the pastors and lay leaders whose responsibility is to teach, guide, and protect the people of God. As Paul warned the Ephesian elders, "I know that after my departure savage wolves will come in among you, not sparing the flock; and from among your own selves men will arise, speaking perverse things, to draw away the disciples after them" (Acts 20:29-30). False teachers are a given, and it is up to the leadership to be on the lookout for them.

But there is also a sense in which the people must share some of the blame. God's Word is available to them as well, and they cannot follow their spiritual leadership blindly. Those who have been built up and strengthened in God's Word are able to discern truth from error and thus have a duty, for their own spiritual welfare, to be sure their leaders measure up to the standard of Scripture.

All believers must act as guardians of the truth. As Paul discussed the privilege of Israel's identity he said, "What advantage has the Jew? Or what is the benefit of circumcision? Great in every respect. First of all, that they were entrusted with the oracles of God" (Rom. 3:1-2). God's primary gift to Israel was His Word. The church is in the same position, for he has entrusted us with the guarding and communicating of His truth.

Unity and Doctrinal Integrity

Before the church can ever fulfill God's pattern for it in this world, all believers must be committed to doctrinal integrity. The apostle Paul stated as much when he said that one of the roles of the pastor-teacher was to build up ". . . the body of Christ; until we all attain to the unity of the faith" (Eph. 4:12-13). By "faith" Paul is not referring to the act of belief or of obedience, but to the body of Christian truth—to Christian doctrine. The faith is the content of the Gospel in its most complete form.

Much has been made in recent years regarding the need to unify the church, and as a result we have witnessed within evangelical circles the inclusion of all sorts of religions and cults. But that's not the unity God desires for His church. Unity of the faith is impossible unless it is built on the foundation of commonly held truth. Jesus prayed, "Sanctify them in the truth; Thy word is truth. . . . And for their sakes I sanctify Myself, that they themselves also may be sanctified in truth. I do not ask in behalf of these alone, but for those also who believe in Me through their word; that they all may be one" (John 17:17-21, emphasis added). Unity is possible only as a result of believers being sanctified in the truth. Fellowship that neglects or disparages the crucial doctrines of the faith is not Christian unity; it is ungodly compromise. (For a complete discussion of this issue, see my book Reckless Faith [Wheaton, Ill.: Crossway Books, 1994].)

God's truth is not fragmented and divided against itself. But when His people are, they are living apart from His truth and apart from the faith of right knowledge and understanding. Only a biblically equipped, faithfully serving, and spiritually maturing church can attain to the unity of the faith. Any other unity will exist only on a purely human level and will be separate from and in constant conflict with the unity of the faith. Unity cannot exist in the church apart from doctrinal integrity.

Guardians of the Truth

Today the church exists in a world predicted by the apostle Paul, who told Timothy, "The time will come when they will not endure sound doctrine" (2 Tim. 4:3). Throughout history the true church remained faithful to the truth in the midst of persecution from the outside and false teaching on the inside. We have received that legacy from those who have gone before. Our only means of counteracting the current trend of doctrinal compromise is a renewed effort toward guarding, proclaiming, and handing down the truth unadulterated to the next generation of believers.

Like today's church, the believers in first-century Ephesus faced the temptation to compromise the truth of God's Word. Ephesus was a fervently pagan city, site of the temple of the goddess Diana (Artemis), one of the Seven Wonders of the Ancient World. Having ministered there for three years, Paul was well aware of the pressures and temptations to compromise or abandon the truth. His letters to Timothy, who was serving as the pastor of the church of Ephesus, are filled with exhortations to live, proclaim, and guard the truth.

In one of those passages of exhortation, Paul establishes the mission of the church with the following imagery: the church is "the pillar and support of the truth" (1 Tim. 3:15). Paul borrowed that imagery from the pillars of the Temple of Diana—all 127 of them. Just as those pillars supported the massive roof of the temple, so the church is the foundation and pillar that holds up the truth. As the foundation and pillars of the Temple of Diana were a testimony to the error of pagan false religion, so the church is to be a testimony to God's truth. That is the church's mission in the world.

Every church has the solemn responsibility to steadfastly uphold the truth of God's Word. The church does not invent the truth, and alters it only at the cost of judgment. God has entrusted the church with the stewardship of Scripture, and its duty is to support and safeguard the Word as the most precious possession on earth. Churches that tamper with, misrepresent, depreciate, or abandon biblical truth destroy their only reason for existing and experience impotence and judgment.

How to Safeguard the Truth

Although it is the collective responsibility of every local church to support the Word, that can't happen unless each individual believer is committed to that duty. There are several ways to do that.

Believe it. Paul gave the following testimony before Felix, the Roman governor of Judea: "I do serve the God of our fathers, believing everything that is in accordance with the Law, and that is written in the Prophets" (Acts 24:14). His belief in God's Word extended to the New Testament. He wrote the Corinthians, "We also believe, therefore also we speak" (2 Cor. 4:13). The many exhortations to hear the Word also refer to hearing with faith. Jesus said, "He who hears My word, and believes Him who sent Me, has eternal life, and does not come into judgment, but has passed out of death into life" (John 5:24). You cannot uphold the Word if you do not hear it and believe.

Memorize it. The psalmist wrote, "Thy word I have treasured in my heart, that I may not sin against Thee" (Ps. 119:11). It is not enough to hear the Word—it must be hidden away in your memory. Only then will you "always [be] ready to make a defense to every one who asks you to give an account for the hope that is in you" (1 Pet. 3:15).

Meditate on it. Joshua 1:8 says, "This book of the law shall not depart from your mouth, but you shall meditate on it day and night, so that you may be careful to do according to all that is written in it; for then you will make your way prosperous, and then you will have success." The psalmist also professes, "O how I love Thy law! It is my meditation all the day" (Ps. 119:97).

Study it. Paul urged Timothy to "be diligent to present yourself approved to God as a workman who does not need to be ashamed, handling accurately the word of truth" (2 Tim. 2:15).

Obey it. Jesus said, "Blessed are those who hear the word of God, and observe it" (Luke 11:28), and "If you abide in My word, then you are truly disciples of Mine" (John 8:31). It does little good to hear the Word, memorize it, meditate on it, and study it if you don't obey it.

Defend it. Paul told the Philippians that he was "appointed for the defense of the gospel" (Phil. 1:16). The truth will always be attacked, and you must be ready to defend it with great vigor. That's why Jude said, "Contend earnestly for the faith which was once for all delivered to the saints" (v. 3). The Greek word translated "contend earnestly" is *epagōnizō*. It includes the Greek word *agōn*, from which we get the English word *agony*. *Agōn* originally referred to a stadium. When we enter the stadium to engage in spiritual warfare, we must battle for the purity of the faith.

Live it. Paul reminded Titus that believers are to "adorn the doctrine of God our Savior in every respect" (Titus 2:10). Having a mind controlled by the Word of God produces godly behavior (Col. 3:16).

Proclaim it. In obedience to our Lord's command, we are to "go . . . and make disciples of all the nations, baptizing them in the name of the Father and the Son and the Holy Spirit, teaching them to observe all that I commanded you" (Matt. 28:19-20). Paul charged Timothy to "preach the word; be ready in season and out of season; reprove, rebuke, exhort, with great patience and instruction" (2 Tim. 4:2). The apostle wrote to Titus that God "at the proper time manifested . . . His Word, in the proclamation with which I was entrusted according to the commandment of God our Savior" (Titus 1:3). "Proclamation" translates *kērugma*, which referred to the message a herald would pronounce on behalf of the ruler or town council under which he served. In the New Testament this term (often rendered "preaching") is always used for the public proclamation of God's Word, which brings men to saving faith, builds them up in divine truth, and strengthens them for godly living.

What a privilege we have to support the truth given to us by our Lord. May each one of us be faithful in that duty daily and, in the process of upholding the integrity of God's Word, establish our own integrity as well.

PROCLAIMING THE TRUTH

The Essence of the Proclamation

The Word of God is a vast, inexhaustible storehouse of spiritual truth. Out of all that truth, what is the most essential for the church to uphold and proclaim? Paul gives the answer in 1 Timothy 3:16: "He who was revealed in the flesh, was vindicated in the Spirit, beheld by angels, proclaimed among the nations, believed on in the world, taken up in glory." The message we proclaim is none other than Jesus Christ; He is the core of what we teach and preach.

Today it is not uncommon to hear evangelical preachers and teachers claim that the simple biblical gospel is not relevant to modern man. They say it needs to be bolstered and adorned by various cultural adaptations to make it more attractive and acceptable. How presumptuous it is to think that an imperfect, sinful human instrument could improve on God's own message for bringing men to Himself. When the Gospel is clearly preached to sinful men and women, at some point the Holy Spirit will regenerate those whom God has chosen, and they will believe and enter into the full benefit of their election.

The apostle Paul knew that the saving faith he was called to preach could never be produced or enhanced by his own wisdom, cleverness, or persuasiveness. To the worldly church at Corinth he wrote:

> *We preach Christ crucified, to Jews a stumbling block, and to Gentiles foolishness, but to those who are the called, both Jews and Greeks, Christ the power of God and the wisdom of God. Because the foolishness of God is wiser than men, and the weakness of God is stronger than men. . . . And when I came to you, brethren, I did not come with superiority of speech or of wisdom, proclaiming to you the testimony of God. For I determined to know nothing among you except Jesus Christ, and Him crucified.*
>
> —*1 Cor. 1:23-25; 2:1-2*

The simple but infinitely powerful truth of the Gospel of "Jesus Christ, and Him crucified" will never fail to elicit saving faith at the appropriate time in those chosen by God.

The only source of this monumental truth, the one true message about God, is manifested in His Word (Titus 1:3). How could any preacher or teacher who names Christ as His Lord and Savior proclaim anything other than God's Word? Whatever truth we need for evangelism is found in His Word—it is the only seed that gives eternal life (1 Pet. 1:23). Whatever truth we need to edify believers is found in His Word (cf. 1 Pet. 2:1-2). Those absolute truths and all others related to spiritual life are found there and nowhere else.

Loyalty in Leadership

While the following is a responsibility for all Christians, it has particular ramifications for those of you who are or who are seeking to become pastors or elders. The foundation for effective teaching of God's Word is your own understanding of and obedience to that revelation. Therefore, you must be unwaveringly loyal to Scripture.

Paul wrote Titus to be "holding fast the faithful word which is in accordance with the teaching" (Titus 1:9). "Holding fast" means "to strongly cling or adhere to something or someone." Thus you are to cling to the faithful Word with fervent devotion and unflagging diligence. In a word, you are to love it. It is your spiritual nourishment. You are to be "constantly nourished on the words of the faith and of the sound doctrine" (1 Tim. 4:6). That involves commitment to the authority and sufficiency of God's Word as the only source of moral and spiritual truth.

Leadership in the church is not built on an individual's natural abilities, education, common sense, or human wisdom. It is built on his knowledge and understanding of Scripture, his allegiance to it, and his submission to the Holy Spirit's applying the truths of God's Word in his heart and life. A man who is not clinging to God's Word and committed to live it is not prepared to preach it or teach it. The truth of the Word must be woven into the very fabric of his thinking and living. Only then does the power of the leader's integrity make an impact on those to whom he ministers.

Those who fail to be loyal to Scripture are largely responsible for the superficial, self-elevating preaching and teaching in many evangelical churches. That failure is the real culprit that has led so many to be converted to what they consider relevancy and therefore to preach a pampering psychology or a diluted gospel.

But the faithful pastor, like Ezra, will "set his heart to study the law of the LORD, and to practice it, and to teach His statutes and ordinances" (Ezra 7:10). He knows that the Bible is not a resource for truth but is the divinely revealed source of truth. It is not a supplementary text but the only text. Its truths are not optional but mandatory. The pastor's purpose is not to make Scripture relevant to his people but to enable them to understand doctrine, which becomes the foundation of their spiritual living.

LIVING THE TRUTH

Effective living cannot occur without a solid understanding of Christian doctrine. That's why in Titus 1:1 the apostle Paul connects "knowledge of the truth" with "godliness." Later in the same epistle Paul says, "The grace of God has appeared bringing salvation to all men, instructing us to deny ungodliness and worldly desires and to live sensibly, righteously and godly in the present age" (2:11-12).

Divine truth and godliness are inextricably related. No matter how sincere our intentions might be, we cannot obey God's will if we do not know what it is. We cannot be godly if we do not know what God is like and what He expects of those who belong to Him. God's truth produces godliness. Commentator D. Edmond Hiebert writes, "There is an intimate connection between truth and godliness. A vital possession of truth is inconsistent with irreverence. . . . Real truth never deviates from the path of piety. A profession of the truth which allows an individual to live in ungodliness is a spurious profession" (*Titus and Philemon* [Chicago: Moody Press, 1957], 21).

In his book *Pleasing God*, theologian R.C. Sproul explains how vital sound doctrine is to sound living:

> We must reject a false dichotomy between doctrine and life. We can have sound doctrine without a sanctified life. But it is extremely difficult to progress in sanctification without sound doctrine. Sound doctrine is not a sufficient condition to produce a sound life. It does not yield sanctification automatically. Sound doctrine is a necessary condition for sanctification. It is a vital prerequisite. It is like oxygen and fire. The mere presence of oxygen does not guarantee a fire, but you can't have a fire without it. ([Wheaton, Ill.: Tyndale House, 1988], 217)

Building a life without compromise can only be accomplished by those who cling to God's Word as the only source of authority and conduct. In the next chapter we'll examine how you can progress in sanctification with God's Word as your guide.

CHAPTER
THREE

IN PURSUIT
OF GODLINESS

J .C. Ryle, the renowned and godly Anglican bishop and expositor in nineteenth-century England, wrote a book of biographical
sketches on the ministries of great British Christian leaders such
as George Whitefield, John Wesley, and Daniel Rowlands. At the
beginning of his compilation, Ryle offers this telling overview:

> They taught constantly the inseparable connection between
> true faith and personal holiness. They never allowed for a
> moment that any church membership or religious profession
> was the proof of a man's being a true Christian if he lived an
> ungodly life. A true Christian, they maintained, must always
> be known by his fruits; and those fruits must be plainly man-
> ifest and unmistakable in all relations of life. "No fruits, no
> grace," was the unvarying tenor of their preaching. (*Christian
> Leaders of the Eighteenth Century* [Edinburgh: Banner of Truth,
> 1978 reprint], 28)

There is a great need in our day for that same perspective.
Instead, many professing believers today think manifesting spiritual fruit is optional—that it is not a necessary and natural product
of genuine salvation. The apostle Paul saw it differently. In Romans
7:4 he asserts, "You . . . were made to die to the Law through the
body of Christ, that you might be joined to another, to Him who
was raised from the dead, that we might bear fruit for God."

Godliness and the bearing of spiritual fruit are so important for believers that Paul often prayed for his converts to grow in godliness and Christian maturity. Steady progress in sanctification is crucial. Without it a life of integrity is impossible. Your desire to live godly will make the difference between your susceptibility to compromise and your capability to stand firm.

THE PROGRESS OF GODLINESS

In Philippians 1:9-11 Paul prays for the spiritual progress of his people. As a faithful pastor, he was concerned that believers in the church at Philippi and everywhere pursue five essentials of righteous living: love, excellence, integrity, good works, and the glory of God. Each of these qualities is sequential; each virtue lays the foundation for the next virtue and helps produce it.

Pursuing Love

Paul prayed that the Philippians' love would "abound still more and more in real knowledge and all discernment" (v. 9). We can infer several basic but profound characteristics of love.

Divine love. First, we know the apostle is referring to divine love, otherwise he would not ask God to provide it and increase it for the Christians at Philippi. Scripture makes it clear that love originates with God: "The love of God has been poured out within our hearts through the Holy Spirit who was given to us" (Rom. 5:5). "We love, because He first loved us" (1 John 4:19).

De facto love. Second, the love Paul speaks about is a de facto love (described by the Latin term meaning "in reality," or "it already exists"). Every believer is given God's love when he is saved. Paul desires all Christians to express more fully the love they already have.

Decisive love. Third, Paul's prayer is for a decisive love—the kind of love indicated directly by the Greek word *agapē*, which is used in Philippians 1:9. *Agape* is the highest, noblest expression of love mentioned in the New Testament. It is the love determined by the will and does not depend on the world's common criteria for love, such as attractiveness, emotions, or sentimentality. This is one area where many believers easily compromise God's standard. They blindly follow the world's demand that a lover feel positive toward the beloved. But that love is based on impulse, not on choice. Impulsive love characterizes the husband who announces to his wife that he is planning to divorce her. His reasoning is, "I can't help it. I fell in love with another woman."

Impulsive love is completely contrary to God's decisive love, which is decisive because He is in control and has a purpose in mind. John 3:16 is not an exposé of God's loss of control of His emotions. He didn't love us because we were so irresistible—there was nothing appealing about us as sinners; He sacrificially chose to love us (John 15:13). When you begin to develop a sacrificial attitude, you'll actively reach out to others and meet their needs without making worldly distinctions as to their merit.

Dynamic love. All believers are to have a dynamic love. The Philippians' love was already growing, but Paul wanted it to expand—to "abound still more and more" (Phil. 1:9). Love that is part of a genuine Christian life, one that's progressing in holiness, will in its essence be dynamic. If we are serious about maturing in our walk with Christ, we'll never be content with a static kind of love, nor the status quo in any other phase of our life. That's how you begin to build a life of integrity: raise your standard, and stop settling for the status quo.

Our Lord never did. He set the standard regarding dynamic love. Ephesians 4:32 says, "Be kind to one another, tender-hearted, forgiving each other, just as God in Christ also has forgiven you" (cf. 5:1-2). The ultimate example of that verse is the humble, sacrificial love Christ modeled for the disciples when He washed their feet. That ought to serve as our motivation to follow His model of service by extending love and seeking ways to minister to each other (John 13:14-17).

Deep love. The fifth aspect Paul requested concerning the

Philippians' love was that it be deep, grounded "in real knowl-edge." Love from God is regulated by a knowledge of His Word, which means it will be anchored deeply in convictions based on truth. Peter exhorts us, "Since you have in obedience to the truth purified your souls for a sincere love of the brethren, fervently love one another from the heart" (1 Pet. 1:22). When we are obedient to and controlled by divine truth, we can love to the highest degree.

Discerning love. Finally Paul prays that a Christian's love be typ-ified by "all discernment." A discerning love will have moral per-ception, insight, and practical application of the deep knowledge to which Paul just referred. Discerning love certainly won't follow the popular adage "Love is blind." Instead, it will strive to determine right from wrong, true from false and to make the correct applica-tion of truth at the proper moments in life.

Those who neglect discernment often become victims of false teaching, spurious causes, and unscriptural practices within and without the church—many times sweeping other poorly taught people along in such errors. So much of that could be avoided if all believers would seek love that's regulated by careful scrutiny and sensitive adherence to God's truth, His Word. Those who love with discernment not only maintain their own integrity but also protect the integrity of the church.

Pursuing Excellence

All believers who are controlled by divine love will also want to seek and approve what is excellent. Hence Paul continued his prayer for the Philippians with these words: "So that you may approve the things that are excellent" (Philippians 1:10).

The English word "excellent" here comes from a Greek word that means literally "to differ." Here Paul goes beyond one's abil-ity to discern between good and evil, between truth and error. He is now concerned that believers be able to distinguish between what is better and what is best—something few professing Christians seem able to do these days. Wisely choosing the best of alternatives over merely the good enables us to set priorities and focus our time and energy on what's really important.

If we want to distinguish intelligently between the good and the best, and make such choices with integrity, we must think. It is imperative that we respond carefully with our minds and not impulsively according to emotion or mood. However, I'm afraid many in the church today are not responding carefully and thoughtfully. Christian writer and conference speaker John Armstrong analyzes the situation well:

We hear popular Christian writers and ministers urging people to think less and feel more. *Experience is in, the mind is out.* The thinking person with an argument is almost always perceived as being in an inferior position to the nonthinking person who has had an experience, especially if the experience is a powerful one which can be communicated movingly to others in the form of a testimony.

John R.W. Stott has written, "Many [modern Christians] have zeal without knowledge, enthusiasm without enlightenment. In more modern jargon, they are keen but clueless." ... We have lots of passion, often of a sentimental and crassly narcissistic sort, but little thinking. Mindlessness is virtually equated with godliness in the modern church. The video age has swamped us, and the result is the loss of clear thinking with more sound bites, i.e., little bits of information (we even have longer "infomercials" now) which move the will almost directly, without prompting serious reflection and thought. Preaching, if we can still even call it that, is aimed at being short, relevant ... and moving. Modern worshipers(?) do not want to think; they want to feel something, and to take away something which will help them cope with fast-paced, busy, modern life. ("Editor's Introduction" [to an edition on the Christian mind], *Reformation and Revival* 3, no. 3 [1994]: 10-11; italics in the original. Stott quotation from John R.W. Stott, *Your Mind Matters* [Downers Grove, Ill.: InterVarsity Press, 1972], 7)

If we hope to succeed in the pursuit of excellence and become people of integrity, we definitely must exercise mind over mood. The following are some more classic passages from the apostle Paul that further encourage us to be thinking Christians.

> *Do not be conformed to this world, but be transformed by the renewing of your mind, that you may prove what the will of God is, that which is good and acceptable and perfect.*
> —*Rom. 12:2*

> *Walk as children of light . . . trying to learn what is pleasing to the Lord.*
> —*Eph. 5:8-10*

> *Be careful how you walk, not as unwise men, but as wise, making the most of your time, because the days are evil. So then do not be foolish, but understand what the will of the Lord is.*
> —*Eph. 5:15-17*

> *Whatever is true, whatever is honorable, whatever is right, whatever is pure, whatever is lovely, whatever is of good repute, if there is any excellence and if anything worthy of praise, let your mind dwell on these things.*
> —*Phil. 4:8*

> *Examine everything carefully; hold fast to that which is good.*
> —*1 Thess. 5:21*

Pursuing Integrity

The solid, unwavering pursuit of divine love, done with Spirit-controlled excellence, will invariably lead us to integrity. Paul's prayer continues to stress the interconnectedness of those essential virtues: "In order [for you] to be sincere and blameless until the day of Christ" (Phil. 1:10).

Spiritual integrity—with its basic components of sincerity and blamelessness—means that a believer is a person who's an integrated whole, one who reflects that fact in every area of his life. I like to explain the concept of integrity with an illustration of the right way and the wrong way to bake bread. If you gather up all the ingredients for bread, toss them into a pan, and put the pan into a heated oven, you won't get bread. The recipe says all the ingredients must be thoroughly mixed before you stick them into the oven. In similar fashion, you can't generate integrity unless you wisely apply (or mix) all the principles of God's Word into all aspects of your life. Nothing about us should be unrelated to biblical truth. We should have no cracks between the areas of our lives, no impurities in the ingredients, for they would make us less than completely genuine. That's the kind of genuineness Paul desires for the Philippians (v. 10).

SINCERE. Paul first uses the word "sincere" (Philippians 1:10) to describe genuineness of character. In the Greek, *sincere* could have had several nuances of meaning. It originally might have pictured the sifting of grain, which in this verse would mean believers need to sift impurities out of their lives and be like pure, wholesome grain.

But another word that can be translated "sincere" derives from two Greek words meaning "sun" and "to judge." If we make those two into a compound word, it would literally mean "testing by sunlight." Commentator James Montgomery Boice explains what that term meant practically to people in Paul's day:

> In ancient times . . . the finest pottery was thin. It had a clear color, and it brought a high price. Fine pottery was very fragile both before and after firing. And . . . this pottery would [often] crack in the oven. Cracked pottery should have been thrown away. But dishonest dealers were in the habit of filling cracks with a hard pearly wax that would blend in with the color of the pottery. This made the cracks practically undetectable in the shops, especially when painted or glazed; but

the wax was immediately detectable if the pottery was held up to light, especially to the sun. In that case the cracks would show up darker. It was said that the artificial element was detected by "sun-testing." Honest dealers marked their finer product by the caption *sine cera*—"without wax." (*Philippians: An Expositional Commentary* [Grand Rapids, Mich.: Zondervan, 1971], 55)

Even as it was wise for customers in the ancient marketplaces to give all pieces of pottery the "sunlight test," so it is wise and necessary for all believers to test their lives for the wax of hypocrisy. When held up to the light of God's Word, the presence or absence of sinful cracks will be apparent. That's why it is so important for us to feed daily on Scripture (Ps. 119:9-11) and to allow our lives to be shaped by its power (Heb. 4:12).

BLAMELESS.   The second key word Paul uses in Philippians 1:10 concerning integrity is "blameless." It describes relational integrity—typified by the person who won't do anything to cause others to stumble. God's Word is quite clear about this. Paul wrote, "Whatever you do, do all to the glory of God. Give no offense either to Jews or to Greeks or to the church of God" (1 Cor. 10:31-32; cf. Rom. 14; 1 Cor. 8).

In general, the integrity Paul prays for all Christians to possess will not only be "sincere" and "blameless" but will also disregard the world's standards (cf. James 1:27; 4:4; 1 John 2:15) and the world's wisdom: "Our proud confidence is this, the testimony of our conscience, that in holiness and godly sincerity, not in fleshly wisdom but in the grace of God, we have conducted ourselves in the world" (2 Cor. 1:12).

The kind of godly integrity Paul had in mind is not to be temporary or fleeting. Instead, we should pursue it throughout our lives, or "until the day of Christ." On that momentous day God "will both bring to light the things hidden in the darkness and disclose the motives of men's hearts" (1 Cor. 4:5). If we have been diligent to cultivate integrity, as well as divine love and excellence, we will have unsurpassed joy on the Day of Christ as the Lord rewards us according to our faithfulness.

Pursuing Good Works

Our pursuit of godliness, if we follow the scriptural pattern, will inevitably lead us from integrity to good works. That is the "fruit of righteousness" in Philippians 1:11.

The New Testament mentions two basic varieties of spiritual fruit that every Christian should produce. One is the fruit of souls won to Christ. Paul refers to them in his letter to the Romans (1:13; 15:28).

The second kind of spiritual fruit is righteous deeds and attitudes. For instance, in Ephesians 5:9 Paul asserts, "The fruit of the light consists in all goodness and righteousness and truth" (cf. 2 Cor. 9:10; Gal. 5:22-23).

The only way we will ever have the strength, wisdom, and faithfulness to produce real spiritual fruit is "through Jesus Christ" (Phil. 1:11). And that can happen only when we abide in Christ, as Jesus explained:

> "I am the true vine, and My Father is the vinedresser. Every branch in Me that does not bear fruit, He takes away; every branch that bears fruit, He prunes it, that it may bear more fruit. . . . Abide in Me, and I in you. As the branch cannot bear fruit of itself, unless it abides in the vine, so neither can you, unless you abide in Me. I am the vine, you are the branches; he who abides in Me, and I in him, he bears much fruit; for apart from Me you can do nothing."
> —John 15:1-5; cf. Eph. 2:10

This is the area of the Christian life where our commitment to integrity is put to the test. (We will discuss the concept of spiritual fruit in much greater detail in the final section of this book.)

Pursuing the Glory of God

All that the apostle Paul prayed for the Philippians' progress in godliness was ultimately "to the glory and praise of God" (Phil. 1:11). That kind of goal was always in view when Paul instructed believers, as when he exhorted the Corinthians, "For you have been bought with a price: therefore glorify God in your body" (1 Cor. 6:20).

A life of love, excellence, integrity, and good works will always glorify the Lord. The word from which we get the English term "glory" (the Greek *doxa*) refers to the totality of God's perfection. When He receives glory, it is also an affirmation of His perfection.

The great incentive and reassurance for us in bringing glory to God is that all three persons of the Godhead completely support the process and are the ones who make it possible:

"By this is My Father glorified, that you bear much fruit."
—John 15:8

We who were the first to hope in Christ should be to the praise of His glory.
—Eph. 1:12

You were sealed in Him with the Holy Spirit of promise, who is given as a pledge of our inheritance, with a view to the redemption of God's own possession, to the praise of His glory.
—Eph. 1:13-14

MANIFESTING GODLINESS

The renowned nineteenth-century Scottish preacher Alexander Maclaren wrote, "The world takes its notions of God, most of all, from the people who say that they belong to God's family. They read us a great deal more than they read the Bible. They see us; they only hear about Jesus Christ" (*First and Second Peter and First John* [New York: Eaton and Maines, 1910], 105). The basis for our presenting a credible witness for Christ to the world is therefore not so much what we say as what we do. Jesus expressed it this way to the disciples: "Let your light shine before men in such a way that they may see your good works, and glorify your Father who is in heaven" (Matt. 5:16).

We have just seen that it is impossible to manifest the qualities of godliness apart from abiding in Christ and obediently following God's Word. But those two important areas of activity require effort and discipline. Paul told Timothy to "discipline yourself for the purpose of godliness" (1 Tim. 4:7). Donald Whitney reminds us that great Christians of the past knew the unsurpassed importance of a disciplined life and that this crucial quality cannot be overlooked today:

> Godly people are disciplined people. It has always been so. Call to mind some heroes of church history—Augustine, Martin Luther, John Calvin, John Bunyan, Susanna Wesley, George Whitefield, Lady Huntingdon, Jonathan and Sarah Edwards, Charles Spurgeon, George Muller—they were all disciplined people. In my own pastoral and personal Christian experience, I can't say that I've ever known a man or woman who came to spiritual maturity except through discipline. Godliness comes through discipline. (*Spiritual Disciplines for the Christian Life* [Colorado Springs: NavPress, 1991], 15)

The apostle Peter put into perspective the fundamental challenge we face in living disciplined lives when he admonished, "Beloved, I urge you as aliens and strangers to abstain from fleshly lusts, which wage war against the soul" (1 Pet. 2:11). Peter calls us "aliens and strangers" because our true citizenship is in heaven (cf. Phil. 3:20). Heavenly citizenship is a great privilege, but it requires us to live by God's standard, not the world's (cf. 1 John 2:15-17).

The opening phrase of 1 Peter 2:11 uses Greek words that liken our status to that of someone living in a foreign country, or of one traveling within a certain land. While we are on earth, our spiritual life places us in sharp contrast to the unbelievers around us, who have different beliefs, values, and morals. We can feel truly at home only when we arrive in heaven: "For here we do not have a lasting city, but we are seeking the city which is to come" (Heb. 13:14).

As people who are on a pilgrimage, we are "to abstain from fleshly lusts," or keep away from the strong desires of our sinful nature. Being saved by grace does not instantly and automatically remove struggles from our life; we still face a spiritual battle against various urges that would lead us into sin (see Rom. 7:14-25). Such lusts can come to us in different forms and tempt us in a variety of ways: "immorality, impurity, sensuality, idolatry, sorcery, enmities, strife, jealousy, outbursts of anger, disputes, dissensions, factions, envying, drunkenness, carousings" (Gal. 5:19-21). In clear contrast to all that, we need to discipline ourselves toward godliness and spiritual maturity:

> ... seeing that His divine power has granted to us everything pertaining to life and godliness, through the true knowledge of Him who called us by His own glory and excellence. For by these He has granted to us His precious and magnificent promises, in order that by them you might become partakers of the divine nature, having escaped the corruption that is in the world by lust. Now for this very reason also, applying all diligence, in your faith supply moral excellence, and in your moral excellence, knowledge; and in your knowledge, self-control, and in your self-control, perseverance, and in your perseverance, godliness; and in your godliness, brotherly kindness, and in your brotherly kindness, Christian love. For if these qualities are yours and are increasing, they render you neither useless nor unfruitful in the true knowledge of our Lord Jesus Christ.
>
> —2 Pet. 1:3-8

If we strive faithfully and diligently, with the Lord's help, to cultivate an inner spiritual discipline, that discipline will reveal itself in our behavior. If we consistently display the highest scriptural standard of behavior and unwavering integrity before unbelievers, it will have an impact on them. For example, a believing wife may through her godly, respectful behavior be used by the Holy Spirit to win her unbelieving husband to Christ (1 Pet. 3:1).

All believers, whether at home, school, or work, should be pursuing godliness and showing forth good works to those around them. By observing such conduct over a period of time, some unbelievers will "glorify God in the day of visitation" (1 Pet. 2:12). That expression refers to the time of salvation (cf. Gen. 50:24; Luke 19:44). In other words, when the Holy Spirit visits a non-Christian and opens his heart, that person will often remember the godly behavior of dedicated Christians and will respond in saving faith.

One of the primary means God uses to proclaim His truth and build His church is godly believers—those who have built lives of integrity through consistent obedience to God. Compromise with the world and its attractions beckons each one of us, but its appeals cannot compete with the reasons God gives us to build an intimate relationship with our Lord, remain steadfast and loyal to the authority of God's Word, and obey God's commands with a loving, willing, and submissive spirit.

———

THE EXAMPLES
OF INTEGRITY

———

RESULTS OF AN
UNCOMPROMISING LIFE

About twenty-five years ago a book titled *The Best and the Brightest* appeared on the best-seller lists. It was a rather lengthy discussion of how some of the sharpest up-and-coming advisers in the John F. Kennedy administration had contributed to American policy-making in the 1960s. Others in government looked to those men for their supposedly wise insights and innovative thoughts on important world issues. Most of those advisers were experts on Latin America, Southeast Asia, or Western Europe. Today, however, their names and ideas are largely forgotten except by historians and other policy specialists.

If we look further back into history some 2,600 years, we find another group who could also be called the best and the brightest—especially in the opinion of the greatest world leader at that time, King Nebuchadnezzar of the Babylonian Empire. Following his first invasion of Judah and siege of Jerusalem in 606 B.C., Nebuchadnezzar took hostage dozens of quality Jewish youths (who were probably in their teenage years) to help ensure the success of his long-range plans for world dominance. One of those youths was especially destined for greatness, and today his name is synonymous with integrity and an uncompromising spirit. His name is Daniel.

Daniel describes how Nebuchadnezzar planned to train the hostages for leadership positions in his expanded empire:

> *Then the king ordered Ashpenaz, the chief of his officials, to bring in some of the sons of Israel, including some of the royal family and of the nobles, youths in whom was no defect, who were good-looking, showing intelligence in every branch of wisdom, endowed with understanding, and discerning knowledge, and who had ability for serving in the king's court; and he ordered him to teach them the literature and language of the Chaldeans [Babylonians].*
>
> —Dan. 1:3-4

Those verses list the priorities worldly men use to fill key positions within government, business, or society. Typically they emphasize image over substance—physical attractiveness, intellectual prowess, and social graces over character, virtue, and morality. That was certainly the plan of Nebuchadnezzar and Ashpenaz, but they got much more than they bargained for in Daniel and his three friends.

INTELLECTUAL QUALIFICATIONS

While this is sometimes overemphasized, Daniel and the other youths would not have been chosen if they had not had the intellectual ability to succeed in their new country. First of all, Daniel 1:4 says that Daniel and the other youths possessed "intelligence in every branch of wisdom." Because they had superior intellects, they had the capability to make intelligent decisions and to discern and apply truth from many disciplines.

They were also "endowed with understanding," meaning they not only knew a lot of facts but could apply them. The Hebrew term translated "understanding" implies ability to correlate facts and draw logical conclusions.

"Discerning knowledge" is the final intellectual qualification, the literal meaning of which is "knower of knowledge." Simply stated, Daniel and the other youths had a superior educational background that prepared them for discerning and handling all the tasks and challenges of their new country. The first such challenge was the reeducation process mandated by the Babylonians.

A NEW EDUCATION

Daniel 1:4 concludes with these words: "He ordered him to teach them the literature and language of the Chaldeans." King Nebuchadnezzar's command to Ashpenaz and the other royal officials marked the formal beginning of the new learning curriculum (one that would take three years) for Daniel and other select Jewish hostages.

Learning New Disciplines

Originally the Chaldeans were a separate ethnic group in the northern part of the Middle East. As the Babylonian Empire expanded, however, Chaldean science, philosophy, and literature became the dominant learning system of the Empire. Before long, Chaldean became synonymous with Babylonian.

The large body of Chaldean knowledge was dominated by the importance of the Chaldean language—an influential and useful trade dialect Daniel would be obligated to learn, along with several other related languages and dialects. He would, in effect, become a linguistics expert.

Daniel's reeducation experience also included the study of what the Chaldeans had learned in mathematics, astronomy, natural history, agriculture, and architecture. At that time in world history, the Chaldeans were the leading thinkers and developers in nearly all those disciplines.

Up to this point, Daniel's new education was probably a positive experience. There was nothing inherently bad about increasing his understanding of math, science, and languages. He may have faced the typical academic challenges that come with learning new subjects and becoming adjusted to different cultures. However, the Babylonians would soon hurl some far more difficult challenges at

Daniel. The ultimate goal was to reprogram his spiritual, moral, and ethical convictions. Nebuchadnezzar wanted Daniel and the other young men to deny their Jewish heritage, forsake God, and set aside the truth of His Word for the sake of the Babylonian Empire.

To accomplish such a radical reeducation, the Babylonians required Daniel to delve into their vast knowledge of astrology, mythology (including legends about creation and a great flood), the magical arts, and their brand of polytheism. In reality, the Babylonians were conducting a sophisticated brainwashing program that they hoped would transform Daniel from a humble Hebrew youth into a polished Chaldean leader.

Receiving New Names

The Babylonians also changed Daniel's name to Belteshazzar. That may seem inconsequential to us, but to the peoples of the ancient Middle East, an individual's identity, personality, and sometimes way of life were all bound up in his name. (In fact, in some older agrarian and nomadic societies, if something or someone had no name, the people viewed him or it as having no being or existence.)

Both the Babylonians and the Jews recognized the importance of names. "Daniel" in Hebrew means "God is judge." The name "Belteshazzar" is Chaldean for "Bel provides" or "Bel's prince." Externally, Daniel's new name suggested he was a disciple of a pagan god (Bel or Baal). But internally, Daniel had the courage to set standards and remain a servant of the true God.

DRAWING THE LINE

Daniel was willing, with God's help, to cooperate only so far regarding his Babylonian indoctrination: "Daniel made up his mind that he would not defile himself with the king's choice food or with the wine which he drank; so he sought permission from the commander of the officials that he might not defile himself" (Dan. 1:8).

The Babylonians culminated their educational program for Daniel and his friends by giving them daily rations of the finest and richest of the royal food and drink. In other words, Nebuchadnezzar and his aides wanted to entice the Jewish young men with some of the perks and benefits available to the upper echelon of Babylonian society. They reasoned that if Daniel and the others experienced the luxuries of their new lifestyle, they would feel a sense of obligation toward their new masters and disassociate themselves from their old customs. But Daniel didn't succumb to their temptation and instead took a stand for scriptural integrity.

Certainly the benefits of the academic training he received were great assets to his maturity. He was able to enhance his knowledge and practical expertise in linguistics and various sciences. And he possessed the discernment to screen out subjects dealing with astrology, mythology, and false religion. He could also tolerate a heathen name, knowing that it was no reflection on his heart attitude toward God.

But the matter of what food and drink to accept was immediately in dispute. Daniel knew well the Old Testament dietary restrictions that God had established for His people, including rules for cleanliness in food preparation and consumption (Lev. 7:23-27; 11:1-47; Deut. 12:15-28; 14:1-29). In addition to failure to meet the dietary laws, there was another reason Daniel could not accept Nebuchadnezzar's meals. Before the food and wine were set out, they were dedicated to Babylon's false gods. The Law of Moses forbade the Jews from participating in any forms of idolatry: "You shall not make for yourself an idol, or any likeness of what is in heaven above or on the earth beneath or in the water under the earth. You shall not worship them or serve them; for I, the Lord your God, am a jealous God" (Ex. 20:4-5; cf. Lev. 19:4; Deut. 5:7-8). If Daniel had eaten any portion of the royal food offered to foreign gods, he would have been participating in a pagan feast, a form of idolatry.

Because Daniel was aware of all those guidelines, he drew a

hard line regarding the king's food. His action constitutes a basic part of genuine integrity and the uncompromising life: *you must draw lines of conviction where Scripture draws them.* If the truth of God's Word is opposed to the world's wisdom on a certain issue, you must align yourself with God's Word.

CHARACTERISTICS OF INTEGRITY

The more we read about and analyze the life of Daniel, the more clearly his personal integrity comes into focus. His uncompromising lifestyle stands in sharp contrast to the way many believers live out their convictions. Many Christians tend to waver and give ambiguous explanations regarding the reasons for abstaining from certain secular activities. But that was not how Daniel approached an opportunity to state his convictions.

An Unashamed Boldness

Daniel did not take the easy way out when presenting his position to Ashpenaz. Instead, he went straight to the heart of the issue and "sought permission from the commander of the officials that he might not defile himself" (Dan. 1:8) as he declined to accept the rich Babylonian food and wine. Thus the young Daniel displayed an unashamed boldness that is an inevitable trait of the uncompromising life.

Daniel accentuated his boldness by using a very strong word, "defile," which throughout the Old Testament is associated with anything that was an abomination to the Lord. Synonyms for *defile* include contaminate, adulterate, pollute, and corrupt. Daniel definitely did not mince his words.

Daniel's fearless statement indicates his desire to elaborate on why the royal food was a defilement to him. That means he explained the basics of the Jewish dietary laws and gave Ashpenaz some carefully chosen words about the sin of idolatry. Unashamed boldness means being thoroughly transparent regarding your stand on issues of right and wrong.

Proverbs 29:25 begins, "The fear of man brings a snare." Most people, believers included, allow themselves to be intimidated by the opinions of others and therefore fall short of the scriptural standard of unashamed boldness. But Daniel and other great figures in the Bible believed that "he who trusts in the LORD will be exalted" (v. 25b).

Scripture is full of examples of how trust in God leads to unashamed boldness. David said, "I have proclaimed glad tidings of righteousness in the great congregation; behold, I will not restrain my lips, O LORD, Thou knowest. I have not hidden Thy righteousness within my heart; I have spoken of Thy faithfulness and Thy salvation; I have not concealed Thy lovingkindness and Thy truth from the great congregation" (Ps. 40:9-10). The prophet Isaiah wrote this about Jesus, the Suffering Servant: "For the LORD God helps Me, therefore, I am not disgraced; therefore, I have set My face like flint, and I know that I shall not be ashamed" (50:7). John the Baptist spoke out courageously during his rather brief ministry: "But when he saw many of the Pharisees and Sadducees coming for baptism, he said to them, 'You brood of vipers, who warned you to flee from the wrath to come? Therefore bring forth fruit in keeping with your repentance'" (Matt. 3:7-8). And every time the apostle Paul was under pressure because of the Gospel, he boldly proclaimed Jesus Christ (cf. Acts 23—26).

It is Paul, in fact, who exhorts Christians to pursue a lifestyle marked by that kind of boldness: "Only conduct yourselves in a manner worthy of the gospel of Christ; so that whether I come and see you or remain absent, I may hear of you that you are standing firm in one spirit, with one mind striving together for the faith of the gospel; in no way alarmed by your opponents" (Phil. 1:27-28). Paul also informs Timothy and all believers how to have unashamed boldness: "God has not given us a spirit of timidity, but of power and love and discipline. Therefore do not be ashamed of the testimony of our Lord" (2 Tim. 1:7-8).

An Uncommon Standard

Believers who live uncompromising lives will invariably set standards that exceed the norm. They won't settle for the status quo. Once again Daniel is our example for this principle: "But Daniel said to the overseer whom the commander of the officials had appointed over Daniel, Hananiah, Mishael and Azariah, 'Please test your servants for ten days, and let us be given some vegetables to eat and water to drink'" (Dan. 1:11-12).

Vegetarianism, or at least semi-vegetarianism, enjoys some degree of acceptance today; but it is not the normal diet for many. Neither was it in Daniel's day. Nonetheless, he chose to eat a vegetable mixture made up of beans and seed so he could set a higher standard.

He also decided not to drink any kind of wine, let alone the king's wine. He certainly would have been well within the Law to drink wine. After all, when properly mixed and diluted, wine was a common part of Jewish society; so drinking it was not wrong. Exodus 29:40-41 mentions wine in connection with the daily offerings. Ecclesiastes 9:7 associates drinking wine with a cheerful heart. And in Isaiah 55:1 wine is actually a symbol of salvation. So, in view of wine's common use by Jews, why did Daniel decide not to drink the king's wine?

Daniel knew that leaders who were committed to an uncommon standard of spiritual excellence would have to make personal sacrifices. Leviticus 10:8-11 illustrates this truth:

> The Lord then spoke to Aaron, saying, "Do not drink wine or strong drink, neither you nor your sons with you, when you come into the tent of meeting, so that you may not die—it is a perpetual statute throughout your generations—and so as to make a distinction between the holy and the profane, and between the unclean and the clean, and so as to teach the sons of Israel all the statutes which the Lord has spoken to them through Moses."

God set a higher standard for the priesthood. The priests were to abstain from wine and any strong drink so they would not be over-powered by its influence and have their judgments impaired. In a similar fashion, other passages contain warnings to leaders about the use of wine. Proverbs 31:4-5 says, "It is not for kings, O Lemuel, it is not for kings to drink wine, or for rulers to desire strong drink. Lest they drink and forget what is decreed, and pervert the rights of all the afflicted." In Luke 1:15 the angel told Zacharias that his son John the Baptist would "drink no wine or liquor." First Timothy 3:3 and Titus 1:7 require that elders in the church not be addicted to wine.

What Daniel decided concerning wine (and non-kosher food) was not at all unprecedented. He wanted to be distinguished from the drunkards and gluttons of the Babylonian royal court. So there would be no confusion between his standards and theirs, Daniel decided to drink only water. Choosing not to drink wine does not by itself make any of us more spiritual; it's simply one way we can set a higher standard and avoid compromising situations and the appearance of evil (1 Thess. 5:22). Daniel's commitment should serve as motivation to all of us who desire to follow the higher road characterized by uncompromising dedication and integrity.

An Unearthly Protection

Scripture is filled with the truth that God is pleased with righteousness and blesses those who serve and obey Him. Psalm 92:12-14 declares, "The righteous man will flourish like the palm tree, he will grow like a cedar in Lebanon. Planted in the house of the LORD, they will flourish in the courts of our God. They will still yield fruit in old age; they shall be full of sap and very green."

Daniel's life fit that pattern as evidenced by how he was accepted in Nebuchadnezzar's court: "God granted Daniel favor and compassion in the sight of the commander of the officials" (Dan. 1:9). Daniel benefited from God's unearthly protection in the middle of very challenging circumstances.

What happened to Daniel is an encouraging reminder that God is in control of everything, including what rulers and authorities think, feel, and do. Proverbs 21:1 says, "The king's heart is like channels of water in the hand of the LORD; He turns it wherever He wishes." Neither Ashpenaz nor Nebuchadnezzar could do anything to change God's plan and blessing for Daniel's life. The favorable response given to Daniel is an example of God's promise in another proverb: "When a man's ways are pleasing to the LORD, He makes even his enemies to be at peace with him" (Prov. 16:7).

The same kind of unearthly, supernatural protection will be granted us if we are consistently obedient and uncompromising in our walk with the Lord. Unfortunately, too many believers worry about what people will say or do if they take a stand on godly principles. So instead they compromise and forfeit God's protection. Once you start down the path of compromise, it inevitably leads to greater temptation to compromise on even more significant principles. It is better to stand firm right at the start in spite of the intimidating circumstances and momentary fears.

A descending spiral of compromise often causes us to forget that God is faithful to His people. Psalm 106:45-46 says, "He remembered His covenant for their [Israel's] sake, and relented according to the greatness of His lovingkindness. He also made them objects of compassion in the presence of all their captors." Joseph (Gen. 39:1-4) and Moses (Heb. 11:23-29) learned to live uncompromising lives in the midst of adversity because they knew God would protect and prosper them. God's faithfulness hasn't changed. If He wants you lifted up to a prominent place in society, at work, in the church, or in any situation, He will do it. Your responsibility is to obey His Word and live with genuine integrity.

An Unhindered Persistence

Even though Daniel, with the help of God's sovereign intervention, made a favorable impression on Ashpenaz and the other royal officials, he did not instantly receive permission to start his vegetarian diet. Yet he was undaunted and exhibited one more trait of integrity: unhindered persistence.

Ashpenaz, the commander of the officials, gave the first official response to Daniel's intrepid request for an alternate menu: "The commander of the officials said to Daniel, 'I am afraid of my lord the king, who has appointed your food and your drink; for why should he see your faces looking more haggard than the youths who are your own age? Then you should make me forfeit my head to the king'" (Dan. 1:10).

While Ashpenaz did display empathy for Daniel, he was not yet at the stage where he was willing to risk all for Daniel and his friends. But Daniel was not deterred. With diplomacy and determination he simply pursued an alternative tack to get the answer he wanted. He appealed to a lower-ranking overseer who was monitoring him and his three companions—presumably a man who would not be as afraid of Nebuchadnezzar since he did not report directly to the king. Therefore, Daniel believed this man would more likely grant his request.

Daniel's perseverance is quite a contrast to what so many display. They give up at the first sign of resistance and rationalize their behavior with this kind of response: "I tried to insist on what was right, but I could see it wasn't going to work out, so I just went with the flow and did what others were doing." Some will even try a few superficial alternatives but soon give up when those don't work out. An uncompromising spirit of integrity, however, never gives up.

The apostle Paul exemplified such a spirit when he was on his way to Jerusalem to be arrested. He persisted in following through with what he knew was God's will, even when well-meaning believers like Agabus tried to dissuade him (Acts 21:10-12). Concerning hindrances and obstacles, Paul told the Ephesian elders, "None of these things move me, neither count I my life dear unto myself, so that I might finish my course with joy, and the ministry, which I have received of the Lord Jesus" (Acts 20:24, KJV).

That was Daniel's attitude. His convictions were firm and settled. Daniel didn't give up just because Ashpenaz didn't honor his initial request. One of the vital traits of integrity is persistence in doing what is right.

An Unblemished Faith

Daniel, in his characteristically bold fashion, asked the overseer to grant a ten-day trial for the vegetarian diet: "Please test your servants for ten days, and let us be given some vegetables to eat and water to drink. Then let our appearance be observed in your presence, and the appearance of the youths who are eating the king's choice food; and deal with your servants according to what you see" (Dan. 1:12-13). Daniel believed God would cause the test results to verify his claims about his diet suggestions. Daniel's holy, uncompromising lifestyle gave him supreme confidence in the Lord. Unblemished faith is a necessary companion to a life of integrity.

Even though Daniel endured a great deal as a hostage, he never lost hope in God. He steadfastly believed the Lord would intervene for him and his friends. The message he was sending Ashpenaz and his assistant basically was, "I'll put my faith to the test, and God will honor my uncompromising spirit."

When we have a pure, unblemished faith involving certain crucial standards—opposing sin and evil, standing for honesty, speaking out for the truth and against error—God will honor that faith. And the source for such standards of righteousness is His Word, which He enables us through faith to obey.

Daniel 1 ends on a positive note and validates the characteristics of integrity we have just discussed. The overseer consented to Daniel's dietary and health test and made the necessary evaluation after ten days (1:14-16). By God's grace, Ashpenaz's aide saw the positive results of the diet. Daniel and his friends were thus allowed to continue with their diet and avoid the compromise of consuming the king's food. In subsequent months and years, Daniel and his companions realized many blessings and privileges in Babylon. They became the elite of all the young men who were enlisted into Nebuchadnezzar's personal service (see 1:17-21).

Daniel's experience is a tremendous illustration of God's sovereign blessing working together with man's complete commitment to the highest principles. Humanly speaking, Daniel's success depended on his own commitment. Divinely speaking, what happened to Daniel was entirely under God's control. The complementary truths of sovereignty and commitment are inseparably linked and applicable in our lives as we seek to live uncompromisingly for Him. We can expect that our commitment to Daniel's extraordinary standards, which are really just God's ordinary standards, will be challenged and tested by the world (cf. John 16:33; James 1:2-3). But we can also be confident of positive results from those tests, just as Daniel was assured (cf. Job 23:10).

Daniel and his friends did not compromise, and neither should we. The scriptural principles upon which Daniel stood are just as real, practical, and reliable for us as they were for him (cf. 1 Cor. 10:11). We'll see that certainty clearly displayed in the next chapter when we examine the integrity of Daniel and his friends as they face fire and lions.

CHAPTER
FIVE

FIRE AND
LIONS

In modern church history, all great missionary leaders and pio-
neers have been men and women of the utmost integrity who
consistently strived to live by the highest spiritual standards. J.
Hudson Taylor, founder of the China Inland Mission (now
Overseas Missionary Fellowship) in 1866, was no exception. As a
relatively new believer in the early 1850s, Taylor became burdened
for the unsaved millions in China. Shortly after the Lord encour-
aged him to consider missionary service, Hudson Taylor adopted
a faith principle, which he wrote about as follows: "'When I get out
to China,' I thought to myself, 'I shall have no claim on anyone for
anything. My only claim will be on God. How important to learn,
before leaving England, to move man, through God, by prayer
alone'" (quoted in Howard and Geraldine Taylor, *Hudson Taylor's
Spiritual Secret* [Chicago: Moody Press, n.d.], 32).

After he resolved to go to China, Taylor began to test his standard, which was to rely only on God for all his provisions. Through
the Lord's help and faithfulness, he was always able to apply his
special conviction and pass the test. One notable example concerns
his salary. Taylor explained what happened:

> That evening was spent, as my Saturday evenings usually
> were, in reading the Word and preparing the subject on which
> I expected to speak in the various lodging-houses on the mor-

row. I waited perhaps a little longer than usual. At last about ten o'clock, there being no interruption of any kind, I put on my overcoat and was preparing to leave for home, rather thankful to know that by that time I should have to let myself in with the latchkey, as my landlady retired early. There was certainly no help for that night. But perhaps God would interpose for me [with a salary payment] by Monday, and I might be able to pay my landlady early in the week the money I would have given her before, had it been possible.

Just as I was about to turn down the gas, I heard the doctor's [Taylor's employer's] step in the garden that lay between the dwelling-house and surgery. He was laughing to himself heartily, as though greatly amused. Entering the surgery he asked for the ledger, and told me that, strange to say, one of his richest patients had just come to pay his doctor's bill. Was it not an odd thing to do! It never struck me that it might have any bearing on my own case, or I might have felt embarrassed. Looking at it simply from the position of an uninterested spectator, I also was highly amused that a man rolling in wealth should come after ten o'clock at night to pay a bill which he could any day have met by a check with the greatest ease. It appeared that, somehow or other, he could not rest with this on his mind, and had been constrained to come at that unusual hour to discharge his liability.

The account was duly receipted in the ledger and Dr. Hardey was about to leave, when suddenly he turned and handing me some of the banknotes just received, said to my surprise and thankfulness:

"By the by, Taylor, you might as well take these notes. I have no change, but can give you the balance next week."

Again I was left, my feelings undiscovered, to go back to my little closet and praise the Lord with a joyful heart that after all I might go to China. (*Hudson Taylor's Spiritual Secret*, 41-42)

That story actually marked the happy ending to an entire week in which Hudson Taylor's internal integrity was tested. On several

occasions he was greatly tempted to exchange his resolve of waiting on the Lord for the opportunity to meet his financial obligations. Because his salary was overdue and he was running out of
money, Taylor could easily have taken control of the situation and
simply reminded his boss about the pay he was due. But he chose
to stand by his conviction, and God rewarded him for doing so. The
lesson for us from this account is not that we should necessarily
adopt Hudson Taylor's identical convictions concerning monetary
provision, or that all our prayers will be answered just when and
how we expect, and not that God will automatically spare us from
difficulties throughout our lives. However, we can learn from
Taylor's example how God values discipline and consistency in all
matters of personal integrity. In the long run the Lord rewards
those who are unwilling to deviate from the path He has called
them to: "For the LORD God is a sun and shield; the LORD gives
grace and glory; no good thing does He withhold from those who
walk uprightly. O Lord of hosts, how blessed is the man who trusts
in Thee!" (Ps. 84:11-12).

INTEGRITY TESTED BY FIRE

In the previous chapter we focused on Daniel's example of an
uncompromising life and made brief mention of his three friends
and fellow hostages in Babylon—Shadrach, Meshach, and Abed-
nego. They are also outstanding examples of genuine integrity
because they followed Daniel's lead and did not compromise
their convictions. There is another well-known account from the
book of Daniel that adds further to their legacy of steadfast
integrity—their experience in the fiery furnace. There they were
confronted by a far more serious dilemma than the previous one.
Regarding diet, idolatry was a secondary issue; this time it was *the*
issue. These three young men (they are no longer teenagers by
this time) knew that God's law said idolatry was a sin (Ex. 20:2-6;
Deut. 4:15-19).

Integrity Challenged

Trouble began for Shadrach, Meshach, and Abed-nego when King Nebuchadnezzar had a dream (Dan. 2:31-35). He saw images of a huge, imposing statue with a solid gold head and a body and feet composed of silver, bronze, iron, and clay. The gold head represented Nebuchadnezzar's own head (v. 38) and so captivated him that he built a real-life gold statue of himself (3:1).

The gigantic statue was a grandiose, totally self-serving project for Nebuchadnezzar. He was merely doing what all unbelievers do: worshiping himself and in effect putting himself above God. The king demanded that all his subjects bow down and worship before the statue—and they did, except for Daniel's three friends. They maintained their integrity and remained firmly committed to the true God and His law, even at the risk of death: "Whoever does not fall down and worship shall immediately be cast into the midst of a furnace of blazing fire" (Dan. 3:6).

Integrity Brings Persecution

By standing firmly for what was right and not compromising, Shadrach, Meshach, and Abed-nego opened themselves to vicious opposition and persecution from the Babylonians. Many of the lower-ranking Babylonian court officials already resented Daniel and his friends for receiving some of the choicest government positions (cf. Dan. 2:48-49). Now there was even more reason to speak out against the three: "There are certain Jews whom you have appointed over the administration of the province of Babylon, namely Shadrach, Meshach, and Abed-nego. These men, O king, have disregarded you; they do not serve your gods or worship the golden image which you have set up" (3:12).

The king was enraged when he heard that report, and he ordered the three men to appear before him (v. 13). As if they didn't have to withstand enough pressure in refusing to follow the crowd that worshiped the statue, the three were now subjected to the desperate, prideful attempt of jealous officials to force them to obey Nebuchadnezzar's edict (vv. 14-15).

For the most part, Daniel's colleagues remained quiet in the face of the king's malicious posturing and intimidation. Their quiet strength of character stands as a greater example of integrity than the most erudite, logical, outspoken response could have been. Their silence was their humble admission that they were indeed guilty of not bowing down to the idolatrous statue. The only response they deemed necessary is one of the most courageous statements of faith in all of Scripture: "If it be so, our God whom we serve is able to deliver us from the furnace of blazing fire; and He will deliver us out of your hand, O king. But even if He does not, let it be known to you, O king, that we are not going to serve your gods or worship the golden image that you have set up" (vv. 17-18).

Integrity Yields Righteousness

The principle of an uncommonly high standard displayed in Daniel's life was also evident in the lives of Shadrach, Meshach, and Abed-nego. Their standard of loyalty and love for the Lord was so high that they were able to stand in the midst of a huge crowd on the plain of Dura, all of whom were bowing down to the golden image. Their integrity of faith was strong enough to resist the kind of peer pressure that so often persuades believers to acquiesce to the wishes of the group.

Their being able to resist in such a manner is testimony to their standard of righteousness, which was solidly based on what God's Word says about purity of conduct (cf. Ps. 119:11). They knew that what happened to their bodies wasn't important, just as long as their souls remained faithful to the Lord. As Job asserted, "Though He slay me, I will hope in Him" (Job 13:15).

The resolve of Shadrach, Meshach, and Abed-nego was soon put to the ultimate test in the fiery furnace, thanks to Nebuchadnezzar's furious, obstinate reaction to their strong stand for truth: "Nebuchadnezzar was filled with wrath, and his facial expression was altered toward Shadrach, Meshach and Abed-nego. He answered by giving orders to heat the furnace seven times more than it was usually heated" (v. 19). Now their only hope of being spared death was God's intervening and granting them deliverance from within the furnace. Perhaps they recalled God's words through the prophet Isaiah, "When you walk through the fire, you will not be scorched, nor will the flame burn you" (43:2).

Daniel 3:20-23 describes what happened next:

> He commanded certain valiant warriors who were in his army to tie up Shadrach, Meshach and Abed-nego, in order to cast them into the furnace of blazing fire. Then these men were tied up in their trousers, their coats, their caps and their other clothes, and were cast into the midst of the furnace of blazing fire. For this reason, because the king's command was urgent and the furnace had been made extremely hot, the flame of the fire slew those men who carried up Shadrach, Meshach and Abed-nego. But these three men, Shadrach, Meshach and Abed-nego, fell into the midst of the furnace of blazing fire still tied up.

Integrity Brings Reward

The Lord sovereignly and graciously rewarded the unwavering faith and commitment of these three men by miraculously coming to their aid. After the three were mercilessly thrown into the furnace, the king was shocked by what happened next: "Nebuchadnezzar the king was astounded and stood in haste; he responded and said to his high officials, 'Was it not three men we cast bound into the midst of the fire?' They answered and said to the king, 'Certainly, O king.' He answered and said, 'Look! I see four men loosed and walking about in the midst of the fire without harm, and the appearance of the fourth is like a son of the gods!'" (vv. 24-25). The fourth man may have been the preincarnate Christ (cf. Gen. 18:1-3) or one of the angels from heaven. Whoever it was,

God sent him to preserve Shadrach, Meshach, and Abed-nego in the midst of the intense flames.

The outstanding conduct of Daniel's three companions in the midst of the most challenging of circumstances is again extraordinary testimony to the value of personal integrity based on God's principles. Such strength of character can carry us through all of life's ups and downs, especially when we know God will be pleased with our response: "For all His ordinances were before me, and I did not put away His statutes from me. I was also blameless [had complete integrity] with Him, and I kept myself from my iniquity. Therefore the Lord has recompensed me according to my righteousness; according to the cleanness of my hands in His eyes" (Ps. 18:22-24).

The testimony of the three men had the further effect of prompting the powerful Nebuchadnezzar to give credit to God and ultimately to bless all three:

> *"Blessed be the God of Shadrach, Meshach, and Abed-nego, who has sent His angel and delivered His servants who put their trust in Him, violating the king's command, and yielded up their bodies so as not to serve or worship any god except their own God. Therefore, I make a decree that any people, nation or tongue that speaks anything offensive against the God of Shadrach, Meshach and Abed-nego shall be torn limb from limb and their houses reduced to a rubbish heap, inasmuch as there is no other god who is able to deliver in this way." Then the king caused Shadrach, Meshach and Abed-nego to prosper in the province of Babylon.*
>
> *—Dan. 3:28-30*

The expression "yielded up their bodies" is a remarkable portent, especially since it was uttered by a pagan king, of what the apostle Paul said in Romans 12:1-2: "I urge you therefore, brethren, by the mercies of God, to present your bodies a living and holy sacrifice, acceptable to God, which is your spiritual service of worship.

And do not be conformed to this world, but be transformed by the renewing of your mind, that you may prove what the will of God is, that which is good and acceptable and perfect."

Daniel's friends were indeed appropriate forerunners of all believers who endeavor to have authentic integrity. The key to such integrity is not that mysterious or esoteric—it just comes down to consistently being radical, obedient, and sacrificial disciples in the Romans 12 mold.

INTEGRITY IN THE LIONS' DEN

For reasons known only to our Lord, Daniel was not involved in the fiery furnace test. However, many years later God sovereignly allowed Daniel to be placed in jeopardy because of his willingness to be uncompromising in his worship of God. And like his friends, Daniel incurred the anger of jealous schemers who could not tolerate his high standards of integrity.

Throughout his life Daniel continued to impress the Babylonians with his outstanding character. His government service was unsurpassed: "Daniel began distinguishing himself among the commissioners and satraps because he possessed an extraordinary spirit, and the king planned to appoint him over the entire kingdom" (Dan. 6:3). The phrase "extraordinary spirit," although primarily referring to Daniel's ability to interpret dreams and visions, indicates something about his consistent integrity and his superior attitude and conduct in the discharge of his daily duties.

Integrity Brings Detractors

Anyone looking at Daniel's situation as a detached and unbiased observer would be surprised by the officials' bitterness and jealousy toward him. He certainly had no character defects that others could legitimately criticize. Therefore, when Daniel's opponents began scheming against him, they had to be creative in their planning: "We shall not find any ground of accusation against this Daniel unless we find it against him with regard to the law of his God" (Daniel 6:5). In other words, Daniel's matchless integrity led to his being persecuted for righteousness' sake. How ironic that his opponents could find fault with him only by attacking his total commitment to God.

Daniel's enemies eventually contrived to pass a new law that dealt with one's loyalty to the king. They persuaded King Darius, ruler of the Medes and Persians, to issue an irrevocable injunction that would make the king supreme and forbid anyone from petitioning any god or man but him (v. 7). The penalty for violating this new law would be death. But that would not keep Daniel from maintaining his uncompromising obedience to the Lord.

Integrity Forbids Shortcuts

Daniel's superior standards of righteousness and integrity simply would not allow him to bend to the king's new edict, even if that document was strict and, in the famous tradition of the Medes and Persians, impossible to change. Daniel 6:10 says, "Now when Daniel knew that the document was signed, he entered his house (now in his roof chamber he had windows open toward Jerusalem); and he continued kneeling on his knees three times a day, praying and giving thanks before his God, as he had been doing previously."

Considering the circumstances, Daniel could have followed the easy path and become less bold and relinquished his high standards of integrity. But he did not. He could have played it safe and discontinued his daily prayers to God for the next thirty days, but he remained faithful and true to his principles. To give in to the intimidations of his detractors and compromise what was right was not in Daniel's character.

Because Daniel did not deviate from his established pattern of personal prayer and devotion to the true God, his foes soon caught him and reported him to King Darius. At this point Scripture is silent

about any response from Daniel. Like his friends, Daniel didn't need
to present any elaborate defense. His strong faith and trust in God
would see him through whatever Darius might do to him.

Integrity Glorifies God

King Darius must have greatly respected Daniel because he exhibited an active and vocal concern for Daniel's well-being. To keep
from having to punish Daniel, Darius earnestly but futilely
attempted to find some loophole in the new law. But finding none,
the king reluctantly went along with the wishes of Daniel's critics,
obeyed the law he had signed, and ordered Daniel taken to the
lions' den (the means of execution). As Darius did his duty, however, he made this remarkable statement: "Your God whom you
constantly serve will Himself deliver you" (Daniel 6:16). What a
powerful commentary on the validity of Daniel's faith and the
strong impression his life of integrity had made. That suggests
Darius was willing to give credit to the true God because he had
witnessed Daniel's uncompromising life and his excellent government service.

Actually, Daniel did not speak again until after God had delivered him from the mouths of the lions. Daniel essentially allowed
the sovereign course of events to vindicate the Lord and himself:

*A stone was brought and laid over the mouth of the den; and
the king sealed it with his own signet ring and with the signet
rings of his nobles, so that nothing might be changed in
regard to Daniel. Then the king went off to his palace and
spent the night fasting, and no entertainment was brought
before him; and his sleep fled from him. Then the king arose
with the dawn, at the break of day, and went in haste to the
lions' den. And when he had come near the den to Daniel, he
cried out with a troubled voice. The king spoke and said to
Daniel, "Daniel, servant of the living God, has your God,
whom you constantly serve, been able to deliver you from the*

lions?" Then Daniel spoke to the king, "O king, live forever!
My God sent His angel and shut the lions' mouths, and they
have not harmed me, inasmuch as I was found innocent before
Him; and also toward you, O king, I have committed no
crime." Then the king was very pleased and gave orders for
Daniel to be taken up out of the den. So Daniel was taken up
out of the den, and no injury whatever was found on him,
because he had trusted in his God.

—Dan. 6:17-23

Tests of faith and integrity don't usually have that kind of
immediate happy ending. Job was the most honest, righteous man
of his time, yet God allowed Satan to buffet him. Isaiah believed
God, but he was sawn in half. Stephen was a superb deacon and
preacher of the Gospel, yet he was stoned to death. Paul trusted in
God, yet he was imprisoned and eventually beheaded. All those
servants of God, just like Daniel and his companions, lived consistent, faithful lives. Each fulfilled his calling and only desired to do
God's will, whether in life or in death.

From the human standpoint, there is no simple way to measure
the power of a life and ministry that's based on integrity and virtue.
In the next chapter we'll seek further insight into the value of such
a life by looking at one more example—the apostle Paul.

IN DEFENSE
OF INTEGRITY

Charles Haddon Spurgeon, the gifted nineteenth-century London preacher, said in one of his later sermons, "I feel that, if I could live a thousand lives, I would like to live them all for Christ, and I should even then feel that they were all too little a return for His great love to me" (cited in Iain Murray, *The Forgotten Spurgeon*, 2nd ed. [Edinburgh: Banner of Truth, 1973], 20).

Spurgeon was a pastor and Christian leader who clearly loved the Lord and defended His cause with integrity. That fact was never more clearly illustrated than during the late 1880s, just a few years before his death. That's when he was a central figure in a major British church struggle known as the Downgrade Controversy. That doctrinal debate began within the Protestant churches of England (most notably the Baptist Union) when Spurgeon could no longer hold back from criticizing the church's alarming departure from sound doctrine and practice. Many churches and their pastors, which previously had been firmly conservative and evangelical, became more tolerant of theories that undermined the authority of Scripture and its view of man. Spurgeon also observed a deviation from the great Reformation doctrines and the proper role played by God's sovereign grace in salvation. From his pulpit and the pages of his magazine *The Sword and the Trowel*, he courageously and consistently spoke out for the truth and urged the average believer to resist false teaching and stand firm on the fundamentals of Christianity.

However, the tide of doctrinal declension among the churches in Charles Spurgeon's day continued, and he was constrained by a godly conscience to leave the Baptist Union. Shortly after his death in the 1890s, some of Spurgeon's supporters formed a new society called the Bible League to continue the battle for doctrinal purity and practical orthodoxy among evangelical churches. During the months of the controversy, Spurgeon received harsh criticism from his opponents, but he never wavered from his defense of the truth. The following excerpt, preached during the Downgrade Controversy in a sermon entitled "Something Done for Jesus," reveals the true nature of Spurgeon's righteous motives and proper integrity:

> We love our brethren for Jesus' sake, but He is the chief among ten thousand, and the altogether lovely. We could not live without Him. To enjoy His company is bliss to us: for Him to hide His face from us is our midnight of sorrow. . . . Oh, for the power to live, to die, to labour, to suffer as unto Him, and unto Him alone! . . . If a deed done for Christ should bring you into disesteem, and threaten to deprive you of usefulness, do it none the less. I count my own character, popularity, and usefulness to be as the small dust of the balance compared with fidelity to the Lord Jesus. It is the devil's logic which says, "You see I cannot come out and avow the truth because I have a sphere of usefulness which I hold by temporizing with what I fear may be false." O sirs, what have we to do with consequences? Let the heavens fall, but let the good man be obedient to his Master, and loyal to his truth. O man of God, be just and fear not! The consequences are with God, and not with thee. If thou hast done a good work unto Christ, though it should seem to thy poor bleared eyes as if great evil has come of it, yet hast thou done it, Christ has accepted it, and He will note it down, and in thy conscience He will smile thee His approval. (Cited in *The Forgotten Spurgeon*, 205. For a more complete discussion of the Downgrade Controversy and its significance for today's

church, see Appendix 1 of my book *Ashamed of the Gospel* [Wheaton, Ill.: Crossway Books, 1993], 197-225)

PAUL DEFENDS HIS INTEGRITY

Charles Spurgeon's defense of the truth and his concern for integrity was in line with the legacy of the apostle Paul. Throughout his ministry, Paul faced opposition from those who hated the Gospel and wanted to pervert its proclamation for their own purposes. Most of the opposition came from a group of false teachers in Corinth. They accused him of being incompetent, unsophisticated, unappealing, and impersonal. As a consequence, Paul was obliged, much against his normal preferences, to defend himself and his ministry. He did not seek to glorify himself, but he knew that the Gospel and the name of the Lord had to be defended from those who sought to destroy the truth.

It soon became clear to the false teachers in Corinth that if they were going to redirect the Corinthian believers toward error and a false gospel, in addition to getting rich and gaining power and prestige, they would have to destroy Paul's integrity. Since he had established and taught the church at Corinth, the false teachers would have to undermine the church's confidence in Paul if they were going to replace his teaching with their own.

If his opponents at Corinth could destroy his integrity, they could also do away with Paul's usefulness, fruitfulness, and ability to serve the Lord. Therefore, Paul had to maintain his integrity. While he had acknowledged his own humility in ministry—"We have this treasure in earthen vessels" (2 Cor. 4:7)—he also understood the real issue at stake in defending his integrity: "that the surpassing greatness of the power may be of God and not from ourselves" (v. 7).

An essential goal for any spiritual leader is to gain the people's trust through genuine integrity. Like Paul, the leader's conduct must be trustworthy and consistent with his words. But once a leader has proven to be hypocritical in any area of ministry, no matter how seemingly insignificant, he has lost everything he has labored for in ministry and sees his credibility destroyed. That is what Paul feared as he confronted the rumors and lies of the false teachers at Corinth.

Paul used his second letter to the Corinthians, and certain passages in particular, to defend his integrity to the church. Second Corinthians 5:11 begins one of those passages: "We persuade men, but we are made manifest to God; and I hope that we are made manifest also in your consciences." Paul wanted the church to understand and accept his sincerity in all things, as God had.

As Paul began this defense of his integrity, common sense dictated that he not expend any more time or energy in further self-promotion (2 Cor. 5:12)—the Corinthians already were well aware of his consistent character and what he had done. Nevertheless, because of the insidious, persistent, and often vicious nature of his enemies' attacks, Paul outlined several reasons for the Corinthians' reassurance regarding his integrity.

Paul's Reverence for the Lord

The first reason Paul offered in defense of his integrity was his "fear of the Lord" (2 Cor. 5:11). Fear in this context does not mean "being afraid," but "worship" and "reverence." A few Scriptures easily illustrate this:

> *The fear of the Lord is the beginning of wisdom, and the knowledge of the Holy One is understanding.*
> —*Prov. 9:10*

> *So the church throughout all Judea and Galilee and Samaria enjoyed peace, being built up; and, going on in the fear of the Lord and in the comfort of the Holy Spirit, it continued to increase.*
> —*Acts 9:31*

Therefore, having these promises, beloved, let us cleanse our-
selves from all defilement of flesh and spirit, perfecting holi-
ness in the fear of God.

—2 Cor. 7:1

Having the fear of the Lord means holding God in such awe that you are wholeheartedly motivated to pursue His holiness and His service. Without question, that was true of Paul. He was so committed to the glory of God that it grieved him to even consider the possibility of dishonoring the Lord's name. Paul's intense reverence for God was therefore a powerful incentive for him to convince others of his integrity.

People sometimes ask me what's most difficult about receiving false criticism. I tell them that what is deeply disturbing and disconcerting is that the unfair criticism can lead others to believe I'm misrepresenting God. That's what upset Paul about the allegations from the false teachers at Corinth—he knew they were misrepresenting him to the Corinthian believers.

A reverential knowledge of God's greatness is what characterized Paul. How else could he make this powerful declaration about God's attributes: "Now to the King eternal, immortal, invisible, the only God, be honor and glory forever and ever. Amen" (1 Tim. 1:17)?

Paul's life was summed up in the exhortation he gave to the Roman Christians: "Present your bodies a living and holy sacrifice, acceptable to God, which is your spiritual service of worship" (Rom. 12:1). His reverence for the Lord was complete, and he was grieved when enemies of the truth sought to undermine his integrity and threaten his ability to teach and preach. Paul therefore felt constrained to launch a defense of his integrity, not for his sake, but for God's.

Paul's Concern for the Church

Paul's concern for the church at Corinth was well established (cf. 1 Cor. 1:10). And his interest in her spiritual welfare was freshly aroused by the potential harm from the false teachers. He was concerned that the false teachers would eventually gain converts and more influence within the fellowship, leading to an ideological war between their faction and Paul and his supporters. The unity of the church would be shattered, which yields other negative results such as a discredited leadership, stunted spiritual growth among church members, and a hindered outreach to the surrounding community.

Paul's response to this array of threats against the Corinthian church is instructive for all who strive for integrity. Rather than jumping into the rhetorical trenches and answering each criticism and lie of the false teachers, Paul took a wiser, more judicious approach: "We ... are giving you an occasion to be proud of us, that you may have an answer for those who take pride in appearance, and not in heart" (2 Cor. 5:12). The apostle knew that in spite of all the dangers to the church, it was not prudent to mount a personal defense directly before his foes. Instead, Paul armed the people he ministered to so they could ably defend him and his integrity.

In the long run, that's a much sounder method to contend for truth and integrity with our enemies, rather than trying to answer each and every charge personally. As Paul discovered, we can go to our opponents repeatedly and present the best-reasoned, most balanced defense of the truth and our integrity, yet all they will do is twist what we've said and use it to tear us down some more.

We are better off to let our friends be our defenders, because those who have something against us are not as likely to feel the same way toward our friends. The Corinthians certainly experienced Paul's consistent behavior and integrity, so there was no reason not to defend him.

Paul appealed to the brethren in the Corinthian church because he was passionately concerned with their unity and growth. In the end he could leave the results of his efforts with God: "He who boasts, let him boast in the Lord. For not he who commends himself is approved, but whom the Lord commends" (2 Cor. 10:17-18).

Paul's Devotion to the Truth

A few years ago I was invited to speak in a philosophy class at one of the state universities located near my home church in southern California. I began my remarks by saying, "I'm here to tell you about the truth you've been searching for all your life. It is all the truth you need to know."

The students in the class were dumbfounded by my approach. Students in those kinds of classes invariably spend the entire term considering various views of the truth but never reach any conclusions. Quite likely they leave the course not expecting to ever find the truth. That's why I went against the conventional wisdom and expounded the truth of the Gospel.

Whenever you are dogmatic, affirmative, and absolute in speaking the truth, as I was in that classroom, the world thinks you've lost your reason. That's how Paul was characterized by his adversaries in Corinth. His passionate zeal and devotion to the truth became another reason for defending his integrity: "For if we are beside ourselves, it is for God; if we are of sound mind, it is for you" (2 Cor. 5:13). The Corinthian believers didn't need to question Paul's reason—they came to Christ through his preaching, grew in their sanctification under his teaching, and as a result loved Paul and trusted in God. His sound mind was obvious to all. But the false teachers and their "converts," in their attempt to overthrow Paul's scriptural teachings with their own self-centered, erroneous ones, charged that Paul had lost control of his senses.

But the apostle made it abundantly clear that he and his fellow ministers were beside themselves for God. The phrase "beside ourselves" refers to his passion and devotion to God's truth. The term does not refer to a person who is clinically deranged, but it can describe someone such as Paul, who was dogmatically committed to truth. And Paul could be more dogmatic than anyone else because he was dealing with direct revelation from the Lord.

Nevertheless, Paul's enemies persisted in labeling him a dogmatic extremist who was off-balance mentally. But dogmatism has always had a negative connotation for the world, as the apostle discovered on other occasions. Notice what happened when Paul gave an earnest, straightforward presentation of the Gospel before the Roman official Festus:

> *"And so, having obtained help from God, I stand to this day testifying both to small and great, stating nothing but what the Prophets and Moses said was going to take place; that the Christ was to suffer, and that by reason of His resurrection from the dead He should be the first to proclaim light both to the Jewish people and to the Gentiles." And while Paul was saying this in his defense, Festus said in a loud voice, "Paul, you are out of your mind! Your great learning is driving you mad." But Paul said, "I am not out of my mind, most excellent Festus, but I utter words of sober truth."*
> —Acts 26:22-24

Once again the solid thread of integrity was evident in Paul's ministry. He was in complete control and possessed a sound, sober mind. Both at Caesarea before Festus and at the church in Corinth, Paul's message was passionate and zealous because the truth of the Gospel was at stake. But he also knew how to be humble and well-reasoned so that people would receive and apply the truth. In the end the issue was the same—he defended his integrity so he could continue to proclaim God's truth unhindered.

Paul's Gratitude for Christ's Love

Another reason Paul was so concerned to defend his integrity was his thankfulness for the Savior's love for him. He told the Corinthians: "The love of Christ controls us, having concluded this, that one died for all, therefore all died" (2 Cor. 5:14). Paul defended his ministry and offered its richness to Christ as an act of gratitude.

To emphasize the strength of this motivation, Paul used the Greek word translated "controls." The simplest, clearest meaning of this word is "pressure that causes action." The gratitude Paul had for Christ's love for him exerted great pressure on him to offer his life and ministry to the Lord. And the overriding factor for Paul was our Lord's substitutionary death and the application of that death to him. The essence of Christ's substitution is summarized well in Romans 5: "For while we were still helpless, at the right time Christ died for the ungodly. For one will hardly die for a righteous man; though perhaps for the good man someone would dare even to die. But God demonstrates His own love toward us, in that while we were yet sinners, Christ died for us" (vv. 6-8).

The death of Christ is meaningless apart from an understanding of its substitutionary impact. If Christ didn't die in our place, we'd have to die for our sins, and that would result in eternal death.

That certainly should be motivation enough for all of us to strive for integrity in our ministries and all aspects of our lives. After all, everyone who died in Christ receives forever the saving benefits of His substitutionary death (cf. Rom. 3:24-26; 6:8). That's the conclusion Paul is referring to in the second part of 2 Corinthians 5:14 when he says, "One died for all, therefore all died." The truth of our Lord's substitution is both a comfort and a motivation for thanksgiving, for Paul and for us: "I shall not be put to shame in anything, but that with all boldness, Christ shall even now, as always, be exalted in my body, whether by life or by death. For to me, to live is Christ, and to die is gain" (Phil. 1:20-21).

Paul's Desire for Righteousness

The great eighteenth-century English hymn writer Isaac Watts composed the following stanzas about the pursuit of righteousness and obedience to God's Word:

> *Blest are the undefiled in heart,*
>   *Whose ways are right and clean,*
> *Who never from the law depart,*
>   *But fly from ev'ry sin.*

Blest are the men who keep Thy Word
And practice Thy commands;
With their whole heart they seek the Lord,
And serve Thee with their hands.

Great is their peace who love Thy law;
How firm their souls abide!
Nor can a bold temptation draw
Their steady feet aside.

Then shall my heart have inward joy,
And keep my face from shame,
When all Thy statutes I obey,
And honor all Thy Name.

Those words, based on Psalm 119:1, could easily have been uttered by the apostle Paul as a way of declaring his all-out desire to live righteously. His desire flowed logically from his tremendous gratitude for Christ's love and was another reason he so vigorously defended his integrity to the Corinthians. Paul told them, "He died for all, that they who live should no longer live for themselves, but for Him who died and rose again on their behalf" (2 Cor. 5:15).

In defending his integrity, Paul wanted the Corinthians to know that his old, self-centered life was finished. Against all the distorted accusations from the false teachers, he wanted his brethren to be persuaded that his motives in ministry were completely pure. And Paul had a strong case because, by God's grace, he was without self-promotion, self-aggrandizement, pride, or greed as he labored to plant and nourish local churches among the people of Asia Minor.

The Corinthians should never have doubted Paul's integrity. He had already instructed them about the spiritual lifestyle they ought to adopt: "Whether, then, you eat or drink or whatever you do, do all to the glory of God. Give no offense either to Jews or to Greeks or to the church of God; just as I also please all men in all things, not seeking my own profit, but the profit of the many, that they may be saved. Be imitators of me, just as I also am of Christ" (1 Cor. 10:31—11:1).

Paul's beliefs and motivations had not changed, no matter what his hypocritical opponents were accusing him of. He still lived for Christ and for the sake of righteousness, not for himself. Any other standard was unacceptable to him.

So Paul defended his integrity because he desired to live boldly for the Lord and didn't want anyone to think his motivation in life was anything less than that. Paul's example should be an encouragement to all of us to cultivate and defend our integrity, because without it we can't minister effectively for the Lord.

Paul's Burden for the Lost

Paul was extremely passionate when it came to reaching the lost for Christ. Seeing people converted by the sovereign power of the gospel message was the ultimate reason for him to continue in ministry. Paul's burden for the lost, therefore, is the last of his reasons for defending his integrity.

Acts 17:16-17 illustrates the intensity of Paul's evangelistic burden: "Now while Paul was waiting for them at Athens, his spirit was being provoked within him as he was beholding the city full of idols. So he was reasoning in the synagogue with the Jews and the God-fearing Gentiles, and in the market place every day with those who happened to be present."

Paul writes about his passion for the unsaved in Romans 1:13-16:

I do not want you to be unaware, brethren, that often I have planned to come to you (and have been prevented thus far) in order that I might obtain some fruit [converts] among you also, even as among the rest of the Gentiles. I am under obligation both to Greeks and to barbarians, both to the wise and to the foolish. Thus, for my part, I am eager to preach the gospel to you also who are in Rome. For I am not ashamed of

the gospel, for it is the power of God for salvation to every one
who believes, to the Jew first and also to the Greek.

Later in his letter to the Roman believers, in perhaps the most
telling statements he ever wrote about his burden for lost souls,
Paul said:

I am telling the truth in Christ, I am not lying, my conscience
bearing me witness in the Holy Spirit, that I have great sor-
row and unceasing grief in my heart. For I could wish that I
myself were accursed, separated from Christ for the sake of my
brethren [the Jews], my kinsmen according to the flesh. . . .
Brethren, my heart's desire and my prayer to God for them
[the Jews] is for their salvation.

—Rom. 9:1-3; 10:1

As he continued to defend his integrity to the Corinthians,
Paul said, "Therefore from now on we recognize no man according to the flesh" (2 Cor. 5:16). This connects back to verse 15 and
simply means that, since his transformation in Christ, Paul no
longer evaluated people by external, worldly standards. He had a
new priority, and that was to meet the spiritual needs of the people of God.

Prior to our transformation we used to assess others by external criteria only; physical appearance, outward behavior, social and
economic orientation, and engaging personality were our old yard-
sticks. But when a person comes to faith in Christ, he begins to evaluate people by a new set of criteria. Then the central issue we want
to determine when we meet someone is, What is his relationship to
God; does he know Christ?

Perhaps you have a neighbor who is kind and considerate, who
helps you out often and is especially available when you have an
illness or emergency. As is often the case, you develop a warm and
friendly relationship with someone like that. But if you are honest,
you can never be content in your friendship until you are sure he

has a right relationship to God. In fact, the more you build your relationship to your neighbor or anyone else, the more burdened you'll become for his or her spiritual welfare.

Paul gives believers no option but to think of the unsaved and everything in life from a transformed perspective: "Therefore if any man is in Christ, he is a new creature; the old things passed away; behold, new things have come" (2 Cor. 5:17). Paul had certainly experienced complete change in his life—from self-centered Pharisee to dedicated apostle of Christ—and he knew such transformation would happen to anyone who became a Christian.

Is it any wonder that Paul defended his integrity so ardently? If any of his enemies could destroy it, he would lose his credibility and influence in preaching the Gospel and thus his entire reason for living. If only every Christian could have the same passion and purpose as the apostle Paul.

PAUL REVEALS HIS HUMILITY

Time and again as Paul defended his integrity, he risked being labeled as proud by the false teachers at Corinth. Yet such a designation could not have been more unfair or untrue. Paul had already, by the sovereign plan of God, distinguished himself as the most noble, most influential, most effective earthly servant the church had ever seen, apart from the Lord Jesus Himself. Yet undergirding all his strong character qualities and various motives for defending his integrity was the all-important characteristic of humility.

Scripture demonstrates that Paul was aware of his weaknesses and shortcomings. In Romans 7:18 he says, "For I know that nothing good dwells in me, that is, in my flesh." In 2 Corinthians 4:7 Paul describes himself in the lowliest of terms: "We have this treasure [the light of the Gospel] in earthen vessels [garbage pails]." Finally, the apostle's humble self-analysis is seen very clearly in what he wrote to Timothy: "Christ Jesus came into the world to save sinners, among whom I am foremost of all" (1 Tim. 1:15).

There is no more cherished Christian virtue than humility. Micah 6:8 says, "He has told you, O man, what is good; and what does the Lord require of you but to do justice, to love kindness, and to walk humbly with your God?" Humility is best defined as a true and genuine sense of conviction that one is utterly and completely unworthy of the goodness, mercy, and grace of God and incapable of anything of value apart from those divine gifts.

Paul culminates his defense of his integrity before the Corinthians with a thorough presentation of the marks of humility (2 Cor. 10:12-18). In this passage he continues to contrast his pure motives and righteous goals in ministry with the impure motives and unholy agendas of the false teachers. Paul was certain his humility would be convincing proof to his readers of his true integrity.

An Unwillingness to Compare Oneself with Others

The first mark of humility for the godly teacher and leader is an unwillingness to compare himself with others and claim superiority over them. False teachers typically elevate themselves. But Paul had a different approach. He told the Corinthians, "We are not bold to class or compare ourselves with some of those who commend themselves" (2 Cor. 10:12).

Those who invaded the Corinthian church with error used glib speech, a superior attitude, and a hypocritical front in order to appear better than everyone else, especially Paul. But he refused to lower himself to their childish, ego-centered games. In fact, he did not even consider such a strategy, saying, "To me it is a very small thing that I should be examined by you, or by any human court; in fact, I do not even examine myself. I am conscious of nothing against myself, yet I am not by this acquitted; but the one who examines me is the Lord" (1 Cor. 4:3-4).

Paul was concerned only with comparing his credentials with God's standards. He did not use man-centered criteria to boast of his successes. Instead, he was more inclined to boast of his sufferings, such as the sadness, tears, imprisonment, pain, and persecution he endured—all for the love of Christ (cf. 2 Cor. 11:23-33).

In contrast, those who are proud and without integrity will establish different standards for success: charm, flattering personality, authoritarian bearing, rhetorical skills, and mystical spiritual experiences. They invent the standards, measure themselves by them, and commend themselves for superior "success."

Paul's standards were objective and God-centered. The false teachers' standards were subjective and worldly. Based on that simple comparison, it is easy to determine what pattern we should follow in our pursuit of genuine integrity.

A Willingness to Minister Within Limits

The humble servant of God will also have a willingness to minister within limits. That was not the attitude of Paul's opponents at Corinth. They overextended and overstated everything they did in an effort to widen their influence, enhance their prestige, and increase their fortune. They exaggerated everything so they would look better than they actually were.

We don't know exactly what the false teachers told the Corinthian believers about their battle with Paul, but undoubtedly they portrayed themselves as more powerful, more sophisticated, more articulate, and more successful than him. And they had to lie to make that case.

How did Paul respond to those claims? Again he refused to engage in the same dishonest tactics of his enemies but simply told the Corinthians, "We will not boast beyond our measure, but within the measure of the sphere which God apportioned to us as a measure, to reach even as far as you" (2 Cor. 10:13). Paul was concerned with only one thing: to accurately portray the reality of his ministry.

Paul always understood the principle of ministering within limits. He mentions it both at the beginning and the end of his letter to the Romans:

. . . through whom we have received grace and apostleship to bring about the obedience of faith among all the Gentiles, for His name's sake.

—1:5

Therefore in Christ Jesus I have found reason for boasting in things pertaining to God. For I will not presume to speak of anything except what Christ has accomplished through me, resulting in the obedience of the Gentiles by word and deed. . . . And thus I aspired to preach the gospel, not where Christ was already named, that I might not build upon another man's foundation.

—15:17-18, 20

Pride and overstatement were not characteristic of Paul. He spoke only of what Christ had done through him and supported his statements by objective, truthful evidence. God had sovereignly gifted Paul and given him a specific commission to fulfill. He was completely content to preach the Gospel in the Gentile world and found churches and train leaders in those unreached regions. He didn't need to be more important than God intended him to be. He just wanted to be faithful to God's plan and carry it out with a depth of excellence that would please the Lord.

What is remarkable about Paul's pattern for ministry is that he simply followed Jesus' example. We often forget that Christ willingly functioned within the narrow limits His Father established.

First, Jesus' ministry was limited by God's will. In John 5:30 Jesus told the Jewish leaders, "I can do nothing on My own initiative. As I hear, I judge; and My judgment is just, because I do not seek My own will, but the will of Him who sent Me." Second, Jesus obeyed the Father's will according to His timetable only (Matt. 26:45; Luke 22:14; John 2:4; 4:23; 5:25; 7:30; 17:1). Third, Jesus limited His ministry to God's people and to those who recognized their need for salvation (Matt. 15:24; Luke 5:31-32). Fourth, Jesus' ministry was limited by God's plan. He preached the Gospel to a small group of people first (including the disciples) before extending it beyond the regions of Judea. Never did Christ allow Himself to get sidetracked onto other issues, and neither did Paul.

An Unwillingness to Take Credit for Others' Labors

Plagiarism has been a problem in the world for centuries. It is defined as "to steal and pass off (the ideas or words of another) as one's own." A truly humble person with real integrity will avoid plagiarism, and that was true of Paul. He never displayed a willingness to take credit for others' labors.

His deference for others contrasted with the false teachers' desire to take credit for things they had never achieved, such as their contributions to the spiritual progress of the Corinthian church. But Paul could confidently and accurately tell the Corinthians how God had used him in their lives:

> We are not overextending ourselves, as if we did not reach to you, for we were the first to come even as far as you in the gospel of Christ; not boasting beyond our measure, that is, in other men's labors, but with the hope that as your faith grows, we shall be, within our sphere, enlarged even more by you, so as to preach the gospel even to the regions beyond you, and not to boast in what has been accomplished in the sphere of another.
>
> —2 Cor. 10:14-15

Paul did not overstate or claim credit for what was not his. Nor did he flaunt authority that didn't belong to him. He underscored what he had said previously: "I planted, Apollos watered, but God was causing the growth. . . . According to the grace of God which was given to me, as a wise master builder I laid a foundation, and another is building upon it" (1 Cor. 3:6, 10).

Paul was determined to avoid the pride and dishonesty of those who "ministered" in a worldly fashion. He would not go to a place and tell lies about his alleged accomplishments. He would not go into a city and usurp the credit for ministry that belonged to another. Instead, Paul knew that those who truly desired to further God's kingdom would do so through their own virtuous lives.

Romans 15:17-18 summarizes well Paul's attitude about this third aspect of humility: "Therefore in Christ Jesus I have found reason for boasting in things pertaining to God. For I will not presume to speak of anything except what Christ has accomplished through me, resulting in the obedience of the Gentiles by word and deed."

A Willingness to Seek Only the Lord's Glory

A fourth way in which Paul exhibited the true humility of the man of integrity was by a willingness to seek only the Lord's glory. The mere thought of self-glory was utterly repulsive to Paul, whereas those who teach error are willing, for the sake of their own glory and preeminence, to tear up the church and tarnish the glory of Christ.

Paul had already laid out his position quite plainly in 1 Corinthians regarding why Christians should seek only God's glory:

> For consider your calling, brethren, that there were not many wise according to the flesh, not many mighty, not many noble; but God has chosen the foolish things of the world to shame the wise, and God has chosen the weak things of the world to shame the things which are strong, and the base things of the world and the despised, God has chosen, the things that are not, that He might nullify the things that are, that no man should boast before God . . . that, just as it is written, "Let him who boasts, boast in the Lord."
>
> —1:26-29, 31

Paul here reminds us all that if we boast, it must be only in the Lord, and if we seek anyone's glory, it must be only His (cf. Ps.

115:1). That is the essence of humility—the recognition of our basic unworthiness and the acceptance of no worthiness but God's.

An Unwillingness to Pursue Anything But Eternal Commendation

Authentic biblical humility is also revealed in Paul's unwillingness to pursue anything but eternal commendation. In 2 Corinthians 10:18 he says, "For not he who commends himself is approved, but whom the Lord commends."

False teachers commend themselves. But Paul desired God's approval, and he proved that he did not fabricate his own commendation. The Greek verb he used for "commends" in verse 18 literally means "to be tested" or "to be approved." That's what Paul meant when he said, "But to me it is a very small thing that I should be examined by you, or by any human court; in fact, I do not even examine myself" (1 Cor. 4:3).

Paul was not concerned about what others thought of him; the only praise and commendation he desired was from the Lord. That's an important reminder for all of us as we pursue integrity: we will receive God's approval not as a result of our gifts, our skills, our personality, or our popularity, but because of our humility.

In summary, Paul possessed the power of integrity. His motives were pure (1 Cor. 4:5), and he defended them for the right reasons— to glorify God and promote the truth of the Gospel and Christ's church. Paul's humble defense of his integrity is, with the exception of the Lord Jesus Himself, the most outstanding and thoroughly detailed example of Christian integrity found in Scripture. How we can practically model Paul's integrity is the purpose of the remainder of this book.

THE ETHICS
OF INTEGRITY

WITH FEAR AND TREMBLING: THE ANTIDOTE TO HYPOCRISY

The story is told of an eastern ascetic holy man who supposedly sat on a prominent street corner of his city and covered himself with ashes to symbolize lowliness. When tourists wanted to take his picture, the man would invariably ask them to wait for a few moments while he rearranged his ashes so he could present a more convincing image of humility and destitution.

The problem with his actions, of course, is that they represent the essence of insincerity and hypocrisy. The story also illustrates what's wrong with so much of what passes for religion and morality today. The ascetic's humility was a sham. He was devoted only to himself, not to any higher cause or a high standard of integrity.

THE PROBLEM OF HYPOCRISY

To be men and women of integrity, it's vital that you be aware of the danger of hypocrisy. You need to know how much God hates it and strive to replace it with godly living. A code of morality or system of ethics that is governed by hypocrisy is nothing more than a charade or a pretense, a game that many people have mastered in their business dealings and social relationships. Sadly, many professing believers are skilled hypocrites when it comes to conduct within the church.

A hypocrite (Greek, *hupokrites*) originally was an actor in ancient Greek plays who wore a mask that exaggerated his particular role. The word quite naturally came to mean anyone who pretended to be what he was not. The scribes and Pharisees of Jesus' time were notorious hypocrites, and their mockery and perversion of God's truth generated some of our Lord's most scathing denunciations (see Luke 11:37-52).

The Jewish religious leaders were certainly not the original or last hypocrites. From beginning to end, the Bible denounces the practice of hypocrisy. Cain was a hypocrite when he pretended to worship God while actually showing off his skill as a farmer (Gen. 4:3-16). When his hypocrisy was revealed in contrast to his brother Abel's faithfulness, Cain became bitter and resentful and murdered Abel (vv. 5-8).

The apostle Paul warns us that hypocrisy will be especially noticeable at the very end of the age: "The Spirit explicitly says that in later times some will fall away from the faith, paying attention to deceitful spirits and doctrines of demons, by means of the hypocrisy of liars seared in their own conscience as with a branding iron" (1 Tim. 4:1-2).

Scripture always condemns hypocrisy. The prophet Amos spoke for God when he wrote:

> *"I hate, I reject your festivals, nor do I delight in your solemn assemblies. Even though you offer up to Me burnt offerings and your grain offerings, I will not accept them; and I will not even look at the peace offerings of your fatlings. Take away from Me the noise of your songs; I will not even listen to the sound of your harps. But let justice roll down like waters and righteousness like an ever-flowing stream."*
>
> *—Amos 5:21-24*

The Lord rejected such worship because it was insincere and absent of righteousness. The people were more concerned with glorifying and pleasing themselves than God. Many other Old Testament passages echo Amos's concern about hypocrisy (cf. Isa. 1:11, 13-15, 16-18; Jer. 11:19-20; Mic. 6:6-8).

On one occasion Jesus quoted from the prophets when He rebuked the scribes and Pharisees: "Rightly did Isaiah prophesy of you hypocrites, as it is written, 'This people honors Me with their lips, but their heart is far away from Me. But in vain do they worship Me, teaching as doctrines the precepts of men'" (Mark 7:6-7).

In the Sermon on the Mount our Lord had the Jewish religious leaders in mind when he admonished the people, "Beware of practicing your righteousness before men to be noticed by them; otherwise you have no reward with your Father who is in heaven" (Matt. 6:1). Jesus was warning His listeners about practicing a form of righteousness that was intended merely to fool other people or simply to impress them. Such a lifestyle does not reveal what is really in the hearts and minds of those who practice it, and it definitely does not give any evidence of the kind of integrity God wants. Earlier in His sermon, Christ had already asserted that such false righteousness would never qualify one for God's kingdom (Matt. 5:20), and here He quite clearly repeats the warning.

Augustine, the early church father, said, "The love of honor is the deadly bane of true piety. Other vices bring forth evil works, but this brings forth good works in an evil way." Hypocrisy is dangerous because it is so deceptive. It often uses good things for evil purposes and thus becomes one of Satan's most common but insidiously effective tools for undermining the church and the reputation of Christians. The threat of hypocrisy should therefore motivate us to have an even greater resolve to live our lives with complete integrity, in a way that honors and glorifies God.

SANCTIFICATION: ACTIVE OR PASSIVE?

The question is, How can we avoid the dangers of hypocrisy and live a godly life marked by integrity? Has God left us some instruction on how to guard ourselves against it? He has. Philippians 2:12-13, just two short verses, provide the balance necessary to avoid hypocrisy and live a life of integrity: "So then, my beloved, just as you have always obeyed, not as in my presence only, but now much more in my absence, work out your salvation with fear and trembling; for it is God who is at work in you, both to will and to work for His good pleasure."

The apostle Paul, under the inspiration of the Holy Spirit, provides us with the perfect basis for living lives that will be marked by righteousness, free from hypocrisy, and characterized by integrity and humble service. His exhortation to the Philippians suggests the ideal balance between two views of sanctification. According to some, it's up to God to perfect us. Others say our growth in sanctification must result entirely from our own efforts. These two views are known as quietism and pietism.

Quietism

The name *quietism* comes from the idea that the believer remains quiet or spiritually passive regarding his or her sanctification. Perhaps quietism's most familiar catch phrase is, "Let go and let God." That motto is a popular way of saying that any effort on our part is a hindrance to the process of sanctification. We must get self out of the way and let God give us a life of victory over sin.

Advocates of quietism often appeal to Galatians 2:20 and take one phrase, "not I, but Christ" (KJV), out of context. In doing so they clearly imply that the Christian life consists entirely of passive faith and trust, allowing no place for diligence and effort by the believer. Yet when considered in its entirety, Galatians 2:20 maintains the balanced tension between our role and God's role in sanctification: "I have been crucified with Christ; and it is no longer I who live, but Christ lives in me; and the life which I now live in the flesh I live by faith in the Son of God, who loved me, and delivered Himself up for me." We live in the flesh, yet Christ lives in us by faith.

Pietism

The opposing view of sanctification claims that our spiritual perfection is entirely dependent on us. This position was traditionally called pietism and flowed out of the eighteenth-century German evangelical movement that reacted to the dead orthodoxy of the Lutheran state church. Pietism had many good features. It emphasized prayer, Bible study, practical good works, and self-discipline—but tended to get out of balance by overemphasizing self-effort.

People who hold to a pietistic view believe the Christian must continually pour all his energy into his pursuit of godliness. Proponents stress verses such as 2 Corinthians 7:1, "Let us cleanse ourselves from all defilement of flesh and spirit, perfecting holiness in the fear of God," and assert that such cleansing is a duty-bound task that is completely up to us. Such a heavy emphasis on spiritual effort, accompanied by constant reminders that saving faith must lead to works, leads to one of two sinful responses: If our efforts succeed, we'll experience a carnal pride of accomplishment. If we fail, we'll despair because now there is no one to turn to for help since God is not a part of this equation.

God's Word supports neither of those two views. Instead it balances the excesses of quietism and pietism.

"WITH FEAR AND TREMBLING"

Paul was not proposing a novel principle in Philippians 2:12-13. Centuries earlier, King Solomon's benediction at the dedication of the temple revealed his recognition of God's role and our role in the process of sanctification:

"Blessed be the LORD, who has given rest to His people Israel, according to all that He promised; not one word has failed of all His good promise, which He promised through Moses His servant. May the LORD our God be with us, as He was with our fathers; may He not leave us or forsake us, that He may incline our hearts to Himself, to walk in all His ways and to keep His commandments and His statutes and His ordinances, which He commanded our fathers. And may these words of mine, with which I have made supplication before the

> LORD, be near to the LORD our God day and night, that He
> may maintain the cause of His servant and the cause of His
> people Israel, as each day requires, so that all the peoples of the
> earth may know that the LORD is God; there is no one else.
> Let your heart therefore be wholly devoted to the LORD our
> God, to walk in His statutes and to keep His commandments,
> as at this day."
>
> —1 Kings 8:56-61

Notice how Solomon expresses the balance between God's responsibility and our responsibility. First he prays that God "may incline our hearts to Himself" (v. 58). Then he urges the people, "Let your heart therefore be wholly devoted to the Lord our God" (v. 61). If we are going to be obedient to the Lord in sanctification, He will have to point us in that direction. But at the same time, we must set our hearts and will to do His will.

Consistent Effort

Over the years many Christians have been disturbed by the final phrase of Philippians 2:12, which says, "Work out your salvation with fear and trembling." Is the apostle advocating salvation by works? He can't be because in Romans 3:20-24 and Ephesians 2:8-9 he teaches that salvation is not by works. So what is the proper meaning of Paul's command in verse 12?

In Greek the verb translated "work out" means "to continually work to bring something to fulfillment or completion." The Roman scholar Strabo (who wrote in Greek and lived about sixty years before Christ) gives us insight into the word's meaning. Strabo uses the same verb when he refers to the Romans extracting silver from mines. By analogy, believers are to mine out of their lives all the richness of salvation God has so graciously deposited there. By sustained effort and diligence we are to work out and perfect in daily conduct those virtues God has placed within us.

Such a command by Paul does not assume any sort of quietistic position, but it does assume a clear level of commitment and continual effort by Christians. The New Testament is replete with similar injunctions, all of which presuppose responsibility by the believer. One key verse is Romans 6:19, "Just as you presented your members as slaves to impurity and to lawlessness, resulting in further lawlessness, so now present your members as slaves to righteousness, resulting in sanctification." Here Paul says the process of sanctification involves our active pursuit of obedience, by the use of all our faculties, even to the extent of being a slave to God's will (cf. 1 Cor. 9:24-27; 2 Cor. 7:1; Eph. 4:1; Col. 3:1-17). If we are day-by-day slaves or bond-servants to the Lord's will, we can't help but live out with integrity the salvation He has granted us.

Paul goes on to describe the attitude with which we are to pursue godliness every day: "with fear and trembling" (Phil. 2:12). As we live for God, we should have a healthy fear of offending or sinning against Him. There should be a "trembling" (we derive the word *trauma* from the Greek word used here) whenever we consider the consequences of sin. Such fear is a proper reaction to our weaknesses and inadequacies, and it provides us with a healthy anxiety to do what is right.

The Lord wants His people to have a righteous awe of Him. The prophet Isaiah wrote, "Thus says the Lord, 'Heaven is My throne, and the earth is My footstool. Where then is a house you could build for Me? And where is a place that I may rest? For My hand made all these things, thus all these things came into being,' declares the Lord. 'But to this one I will look, to him who is humble and contrite of spirit, and who trembles at My word'" (Isa. 66:1-2; cf. Prov. 1:7). God looks for and approves those who tremble or shake before His Word.

Working out our salvation on a daily basis with consistency and integrity is difficult. And the possibility of failure looms constantly. One of the safeguards that helps prevent failure is the sort of healthy fear, awe, and respect for God inherent in Philippians 2:12. It's not a fear of eternal torment, a despair due to our circumstances, or a neurotic feeling that paralyzes us into inaction.

Instead, it's a reverence that motivates us and puts us on guard so we won't stumble and lose our joy. It guides us so we won't offend the Lord, compromise the integrity of our testimony before unbelievers, or negate our usefulness and ministry to other believers in the body of Christ.

Utter Dependence

Working out our salvation would be useless—and indeed impossible—if it were not balanced by the truth of Philippians 2:13, "For it is God who is at work in you, both to will and to work for His good pleasure." The glory of Christian living is that God calls us to obey and then effects that obedience in us. Our progress in sanctification demands all that we are, but it also demands all that God is in us. In John 15:5 Jesus says, "I am the vine, you are the branches; he who abides in Me, and I in him, he bears much fruit; for apart from Me you can do nothing." When you see spiritual fruit in your life, realize that God produced it: "There are varieties of effects, but the same God who works all things in all persons" (1 Cor. 12:6).

I wonder how many Christians take for granted the awesome reality that God is actually in us—not merely working on us or for us, but truly *in* all genuine believers. In Acts 1:8 Jesus told the apostles, "You shall receive power when the Holy Spirit has come upon you." God lives in us by His Holy Spirit (1 Cor. 3:16-17; 6:19). We can be assured that He did not go to great lengths to justify us and then leave us alone to work out our own sanctification. Galatians 3:3 says, "Are you so foolish? Having begun by the Spirit, are you now being perfected by the flesh?" Obviously, the answer Paul expects to this question is a resolute "No."

According to Philippians 2:13, the twofold purpose for God's working in us is to cause us "to will and to work." That means the Lord wants to energize our desires and our actions.

DESIRING WHAT IS RIGHT.   First of all, God wants us to desire what is right. All behavior arises from the human will—our desires, inclinations, and intentions. The Greek verb for "will" in verse 13 does not refer to passion, lust, or whimsical emotion. Rather, it focuses on intent and inclination—the dispassionate will of one's studied, planned purpose. As Psalm 110:3 declares, "Thy people will volunteer freely in the day of Thy power." God's power moves within us to make us willing to live godly lives, to do and say what is right and just, and to walk with integrity.

Generally, God produces two attitudes in us to move our wills toward sanctification. One is a *righteous discontent* with our present spiritual state. That means God makes us dislike the various sins that beset us. The apostle Paul expressed his discontent in this way: "Wretched man that I am! Who will set me free from the body of this death?" (Rom. 7:24). If God's Spirit produces in us such discontent, we know it is proper, unlike the sinful attitude of discontent we might have toward our circumstances.

Second, God moves our wills toward sanctification by giving us a *holy aspiration*. We long to be purer, holier, more righteous, and more genuine in our walk with Christ than we have been—a longing to be virtuous in our lifestyle and have victory over sin. Such desire may come, for example, while we're reading about a Bible character, either in Scripture or a Christian biography. As we read, our heart underscores our weak level of spiritual dedication compared to that person in history whom God used so effectively. A strong desire to do better, to live more like Christ, then burns within us.

WORK OUT WHAT IS RIGHT. The second purpose for God's working in us is so that we might work. God works in us so we'll be able to do deeds of righteousness. Paul gives us a glimpse of the scope of this process when he prays, "Now to Him who is able to do exceeding abundantly beyond all that we ask or think, according to the power that works within us . . ." (Eph. 3:20). Our omnipotent God can and does accomplish through us that which is unimaginable, beyond our ability to plan or dream.

Philippians 2:13 adds that when, by God's power, we want to

serve Him, we are accomplishing deeds "for His good pleasure." The word translated "pleasure" means "satisfaction." God wants us to do what satisfies Him. Because of our special relationship to God, He takes great pleasure in our willing and working on His behalf.

The incomprehensible truth of verse 13, that God is enabling us to live for Him and is pleased when we do, makes all the challenge and effort of working out our salvation with fear and trembling worthwhile. And it should give us all the encouragement and incentive we'll ever need to live with integrity and without hypocrisy before the world (cf. 1 Cor. 15:58).

THE NEED FOR DISCIPLINE

None of the things we've just discussed, however, will be fully realized in our lives if we do not exercise self-discipline. It's unscriptural and just plain wrong to think we can progress in godliness simply on good intentions and warm feelings regarding the Christian life. The Lord can work effectively only through lives that are disciplined and submitted to Him. The apostle Paul reminds us of how crucial personal discipline is:

> *Everyone who competes in the games exercises self-control in all things. They then do it to receive a perishable wreath, but we an imperishable. Therefore I run in such a way, as not without aim; I box in such a way, as not beating the air; but I buffet my body and make it my slave, lest possibly, after I have preached to others, I myself should be disqualified.*
> —1 Cor. 9:25-27

Only the disciplined Christian will consistently read and study God's Word and then diligently apply it as he allows God's power to conform him more and more to the image of Christ. None other than the disciplined Christian can truly evaluate and effectively challenge the world's culture and value system in the light of

Scripture. Simply stated, self-discipline is the willingness to subordinate personal and selfish interests to God's eternal interests.

It was said of the popular nineteenth-century English author William Arnot, "His preaching is good. His writing is better. His living is best of all." All of us should desire that people would see our living as "best of all." The point is not that our life will have perfect integrity and we will never waver in our commitment and obedience to God, but that the general direction of our daily living will be more and more toward the supreme standard of Jesus Christ.

Our lives will not move in that direction until we place God first in our lives and begin to obey His priorities, and that is the subject of the next chapter.

RENDER UNTO GOD

The expression "The only constant is constant change" seems more true with each passing year. In today's high-tech culture you could add the following phrase to that cliché: "and constant busyness." You would be hard pressed to find anyone in business who doesn't depend daily on his or her schedule books and planners in an effort to control and stay ahead of life's fast pace. Each day seems to bring new stresses and challenges in the home and workplace. In the midst of such a culture, people continually strive to balance their priorities, do what's right, and still find new avenues of success.

That scenario also applies to many Christians. Thousands constantly seek new keys to effective living, both temporal and eternal. Christians run after new books, videos, seminars, and computer software in search of practical, emotional, and spiritual improvement. They seem to have forgotten that the secret to a well-balanced life lies not in programs, activities, or a flurry of self-help efforts, but in a proper, foundational relationship with the Lord.

Jesus taught this principle within the context of a bustle of activity when He once visited the home of sisters Mary and Martha. The story is a familiar one:

Now as they were traveling along, He entered a certain village; and a woman named Martha welcomed Him into her

*home. And she had a sister called Mary, who moreover was
listening to the Lord's word, seated at His feet. But Martha
was distracted with all her preparations; and she came up to
Him, and said, "Lord, do you not care that my sister has left
me to do all the serving alone? Then tell her to help me." But
the Lord answered and said to her, "Martha, Martha, you are
worried and bothered about so many things; but only a few
things are necessary, really only one, for Mary has chosen the
good part, which shall not be taken away from her."*
                                                —Luke 10:38-42

The essential thing, then, if we would be men and women who
live useful and fulfilled Christian lives, is that we put God first.
That is in essence what we discussed in the first chapter. Our relationship with Jesus Christ is the key to establishing a life without
compromise. I remind you of that in this chapter because we need
to capture His passion and perspective on how to live lives that glorify God. There are several practical duties that can help us accomplish that, and we find them in Hebrews 13:10-21. There are four
areas of Christian conduct that, if obeyed, will demonstrate that we
are people of integrity when we profess to love God above all else.

SEPARATION FROM THE WORLD

The first command is that we must separate ourselves from the
world. The author of Hebrews says, "Therefore Jesus also, that He
might sanctify the people through His own blood, suffered outside
the gate. Hence, let us go out to Him outside the camp, bearing His
reproach" (Hebrews 13:12-13).

From those verses we can draw an analogy of the Christian life.
Believers follow Christ's example and separate themselves from a
sinful world. Since Jesus died outside Jerusalem, apart from the old
system of Judaism and away from the sins of the people, we also
should live outside the world, no longer a part of its sinful standards and practices. We must be willing to live apart from the sys-

tem and at times suffer persecution or ridicule because of our allegiance to Christ.

The apostle Paul reminds us that we have nothing in common with the world: "Do not be bound together with unbelievers; for what partnership have righteousness and lawlessness, or what fellowship has light with darkness?" (2 Cor. 6:14). That kind of separation does not mean we should stop all contact with unbelievers or become monastics. If that were the case, we would not be able to minister to those who don't know the Lord. Scriptural separation involves having a different attitude and orientation from the world's, and not compromising our standards to fit its customs. However, our attitude toward it cannot be condescending, otherwise we adopt a prideful outlook.

Jesus prayed that God would give us a right attitude and proper relationship to the world: "I do not ask Thee to take them out of the world, but to keep them from the evil one. They are not of the world, even as I am not of the world. Sanctify them in the truth; Thy word is truth. As Thou didst send Me into the world, I also have sent them into the world" (John 17:15-18). The Father and the Son know that we must live in the world, but they want us to be distinct from the habits and attitudes that characterize the world (cf. 1 John 2:15-17).

Living a truly separated life is not easy. The apostle Paul explains the cost of such a life: "All who desire to live godly in Christ Jesus will be persecuted" (2 Tim. 3:12). Many believers do not face persecution today simply because so few are living godly lives outside the camp of the world. Too many prefer to compromise righteous integrity in favor of worldly prestige. Paul admonished the worldly Corinthians about that and challenged them to follow his example and accept the difficulties of living a separated life: "We are fools for Christ's sake, but you are prudent in Christ; we are weak, but you are strong; you are distinguished, but we are without honor. To this present hour we are both hungry and thirsty, and are poorly clothed, and are roughly treated, and are homeless" (1 Cor. 4:10-11).

SACRIFICIAL LIVING

All Christians realize that Jesus Christ has offered in Himself the one and only sacrifice for their sins. But many of us often forget that God requires sacrifice from us in the form of praise to Him and service to others. The author of Hebrews writes, "Through Him then, let us continually offer up a sacrifice of praise to God, that is, the fruit of lips that give thanks to His name. And do not neglect doing good and sharing; for with such sacrifices God is pleased" (13:15-16). That is another attribute that should characterize all believers who wish to live with integrity—the attitude of sacrificial living.

The authors of the Psalms knew a great deal about the first aspect of a sacrificial attitude: praising God and giving thanks to His name. Here are just three examples:

> *I will give thanks to the LORD according to His righteousness, and will sing praise to the name of the LORD Most High.*
>
> *—7:17*

> *Why are you in despair, O my soul? And why are you disturbed within me? Hope in God, for I shall again praise Him.*
>
> *—43:5*

> *I will give thanks to Thee, O LORD, among the peoples; and I will sing praises to Thee among the nations.*
>
> *—108:3*

Offering sacrifices of praise should not occur only when we receive some blessing from God; it should characterize us at all times and in all circumstances. Paul instructs us, "In everything give thanks; for this is God's will for you in Christ Jesus" (1 Thess. 5:18).

The apostle John cautions us that such speech must accompany a second aspect of sacrificial living, and that is practical service and good deeds to others: "Little children, let us not love with word or with tongue, but in deed and truth" (1 John 3:18). Putting God first in our lives and worshiping Him above all else will, if our faith is authentic, result in actions that honor Him. Mere lip-service to what we know we ought to do is not the mark of a person with integrity (cf. James 4:17).

That most practical of New Testament books, the Epistle of James, demonstrates quite directly that words of praise and deeds of service must go together: "This is pure and undefiled religion in the sight of our God and Father, to visit orphans and widows in their distress, and to keep oneself unstained by the world" (James 1:27). First John 4:20 again summarizes the crucial nature of this point and what it really means if we do not obey it: "the one who does not love his brother whom he has seen, cannot love God whom he has not seen." If our actions do not match our profession of love and praise to God, we have no reason to assume that we're part of His family.

A SUBMISSIVE ATTITUDE

The writer of Hebrews mentions a third key area of attitude and conduct that proves the truth of the believer's integrity before the Lord—submission.

To Spiritual Leaders

In addition to the work of His Spirit, God rules through the Spirit-controlled men who lead the church. Hebrews 13:17 declares how this principle is to work: "Obey your leaders, and submit to them; for they keep watch over your souls, as those who will give an account. Let them do this with joy and not with grief, for this would be unprofitable for you."

God has designed His church in such a way that qualified, divinely appointed men preside over it and, with God's help, determine its direction, teach the Word, and give guidance and correction to the people. Every New Testament church had these men, called elders and overseers (cf. Acts 20:28; Titus 1:5). The apostle Peter provided instruction on how they were to carry out their oversight of the church: "Shepherd the flock of God among you, not under compulsion, but voluntarily, according to the will of God; and not for sordid gain, but with eagerness; nor yet as lording it over those allotted to your charge, but proving to be examples to the flock" (1 Pet. 5:2-3).

Since leaders are commanded to rule in love and humility, then those under them are also to submit to their authority in love and humility. The apostle Paul told the Thessalonian church, "We request of you, brethren, that you appreciate those who diligently labor among you, and have charge over you in the Lord and give you instruction, and that you esteem them very highly in love because of their work" (1 Thess. 5:12-13).

Hebrews 13 adds that the people of God are responsible to help their leaders rule with joy and satisfaction. One of the primary ways we can do this is to willingly submit to their authority. Therefore, the joy of our leaders in the Lord should be a primary incentive for our submission to them.

Jesus made the necessity of our submitting to spiritual authority even more imperative when He told the disciples, "He who receives whomever I send receives Me; and he who receives Me receives Him who sent Me" (John 13:20). Our submission and obedience to the elders in our local church is equivalent to our submission and obedience to Christ.

The Christians in Philippi illustrate the kind of submission to leaders God wants. Since the Philippians held to sound doctrine and were not rebellious to Paul or any of the leaders, Paul could be gracious and pleasant when writing to them: "I thank my God in all my remembrance of you, always offering prayer with joy in my every prayer for you all" (Phil. 1:3-4).

We do know, however, that spiritual leaders are not infallible or perfect. And so we are not necessarily displaying a lack of integrity or sinful disobedience if we disagree with or rebuke an elder in the church. But God's Word does give clear guidelines on how and when this is to be done. First Timothy 5:19-20 says, "Do not receive an accusation against an elder except on the basis of two or three witnesses. Those who continue in sin, rebuke in the presence of all, so that the rest also may be fearful of sinning." Such an action against a spiritual leader should never be done hastily, but only after sufficient evidence is present, and with all humility and respect.

It is far more personally rewarding and spiritually profitable for us if we cultivate and live out an attitude of submission to our spiritual leaders. The Lord is pleased, they rejoice, and we also receive joy. Paul's joy in faithful believers was always related to their joy in obedience: "Rejoice in the same way and share your joy with me" (Phil. 2:18).

To Governing Authorities

An area of submission to God that many Christians don't want to be reminded of is their responsibility to submit to the governing authorities. The apostle Peter says, "Submit yourselves for the Lord's sake to every human institution, whether to a king as the one in authority, or to governors as sent by him for the punishment of evildoers and the praise of those who do right" (1 Pet. 2:13-14; cf. Rom. 13:1-7).

The Lord is the one who has ordained civil authority; so when a believer submits himself to it, he is obeying the Lord. Peter's audience was first-century Christians living under the Roman Empire—a pagan, hostile, anti-Semitic government. If anyone had a reason to rebel, humanly speaking, they did. But it is the responsibility of every Christian, no matter what form of government he lives under, to maintain proper and useful submission to the government for the sake of leading a peaceful life and having an effective witness.

To Employers

This last area of submission is just as vital as the previous one. Peter writes, "Servants, be submissive to your masters with all respect, not only to those who are good and gentle, but also to those who are unreasonable" (1 Pet. 2:18).

The dominant social structure of the Roman Empire was slavery, and slaves were often the subjects of disrespect. It's likely that most Christians in the early church were slaves, and in the majority of cases servants of an owner of a house or estate ("servants," Greek, *oiketēs*). The closest approximation we have to this master-slave relationship today is the employer-employee relationship.

Just as the possibility existed that the slave could have a "good and gentle" master or an "unreasonable" one, so any employee today can have a good or a bad boss. But for the Christian, the type of employer you have is not the issue regarding your submission. God commands all to submit "with all respect." That speaks of fearing God, not man. We have a higher calling; we are to be mindful of God in what we do and say (1:17; 2:17; 3:2, 15). That includes respecting the social order, such as the employer-employee relationship, since He has sovereignly designed it for the sake of orderliness and productivity. Thus we are to serve our employer as though we are serving the Lord.

SUPPLICATION FOR OTHERS

According to Hebrews 13:10-21, there is one more obligation we have in manifesting integrity before God—supplication to Him on behalf of our spiritual leaders. That responsibility flows very logically from our submissive attitude. When we willingly submit to those who have charge over our souls, then it makes sense that we should also desire to pray for them. God is sovereign, but prayer is one of the means He has chosen to use in orchestrating His perfect plan through His servants. James exhorts us with these simple but profound words: "The effective prayer [supplication] of a righteous man can accomplish much" (James 5:16).

Every servant of Christ needs the prayers of those he ministers to. He has human sins, weaknesses, and limitations. If we are not faithful to pray for those over us in the church, they will not be as effective as the Lord wants them to be in His work (cf. James 3:1).

God's leaders face more intense spiritual opposition and temptation than do average believers. Satan knows if he can get leaders to compromise, weaken their stand for truth, slack off in their ministry efforts, or simply become discouraged, he will damage the cause of Christ and do harm to many believers. That's why the apostle Paul readily asked prayer from those he had ministered to: "Pray on my behalf, that utterance may be given to me in the opening of my mouth, to make known with boldness the mystery of the gospel" (Eph. 6:19). If Paul made such a request, certainly ordinary ministers of the Gospel need and deserve our prayers.

The writer of Hebrews evidently was a leader in the church or churches to whom he was writing. And like Paul he confidently asked that the people pray for him and all leaders because "we are sure that we have a good conscience, desiring to conduct ourselves honorably in all things" (Heb. 13:18). He believed with all his heart that he had been faithful in ministry. But his belief was not presumptuous; it was based on his conscience as a Christian.

All Christians have cleansed and purified consciences (Heb. 9:14), which means the Holy Spirit helps them discern what is right and gives them the ability to do it. A good conscience enables us to be honest about our needs with ourselves and with others, which is exactly what the author of Hebrews was doing. He could honestly say he had served well the people given into his care and oversight. Before God he had a right to expect his flock to intercede for him. Bona fide spiritual leaders, those whom God has put in charge over us and who truly care about the welfare of our souls, both need and deserve our prayers.

To sum up, our integrity must include our recognition that God has to be first in our lives and that we have to live in a way that is consistent with our calling. Once we obey our basic responsibilities before the Lord and those whom He sets over us, we become far better prepared to please Him in the essential areas of personal holiness. Before long we'll see ourselves in the following picture of discipleship, described by a nineteenth-century pastor:

> The true Christian possesses such impressions of his absolute dependence and has such view of God's entire right to him that he feels that all he is and all that he has belong to God. And hence his heart in the first place is devoted to the service of God. He has a sacred relish for the duties and designs which he knows every creature of God ought to accomplish. The service of God is no irksome employment, but one in which he feels heartily and cheerfully engaged. There is nothing to which his affections are so strongly attached and in which he takes so much delight as in doing good. He loves the work of pleasing and glorifying his Redeemer, and of doing good to his fellow men. "My meat," saith the Lord Jesus, "is to do the will of him who sent me, and to finish his work" (Jo. 4:34). And the disciple, though far from coming up to the high standard of his Master's example, is in this respect like his Lord. There is a pleasure, a satisfaction of soul he enjoys in the service of God which no other employment can impart. No matter what position he may occupy in the world, he may be a minister of the Gospel, an officer in the church, or a private Christian; he may be a magistrate or a subject, he may be rich or poor, he may be a legislator, a lawyer, or a physician, he may be a farmer, a merchant, a mechanic, or common laborer; he may be a seaman or a landsman, a master or a servant; and if he is a child of God, his heart will be bound up in the work of doing good and in pleasing and serving God. (Gardiner Spring, *The Distinguishing Traits of Christian Character* [1829; reprint, Nutley, N.J.: Presbyterian and Reformed, 1977], 47)

THE RESPONSIBILITIES OF PERSONAL HOLINESS

The late Martyn Lloyd-Jones, considered by many to be the most gifted expositor of the twentieth century, wrote the following:

> As you go on living this righteous life, and practising it with all your might and energy, and all your time ... you will find that the process that went on before, in which you went on from bad to worse and became viler and viler, is entirely reversed. You will become cleaner and cleaner, and purer and purer, and holier and holier, and more and more conformed unto the image of the Son of God. (*Romans: An Exposition of Chapter Six* [Grand Rapids, Mich.: Zondervan, 1972], 268-69)

A consistently righteous life is the showcase of one's integrity because it reveals your commitment to love and obey God. When your behavior is consistent with who you claim to be—when your deeds match your words—you have integrity. Clearly there is a direct correlation between integrity and biblical holiness. And God leads every believer along the path to holiness through the process of sanctification. As Dr. Lloyd-Jones said, that process culminates in Christian maturity as each believer is conformed into the image of Christ. That is true holiness and integrity.

Therefore, if we would be men and women of integrity, we must also be men and women of holiness. And that requires com-

plete diligence and attentiveness toward all aspects of sanctification, including the vital area of *personal* holiness. There are several
key responsibilities all Christians must meet to develop personal
holiness.

SEXUAL PURITY: THE DIGNITY OF MARRIAGE

Today's culture is obsessed with sex more than ever. Even though
there is the distinct possibility of contracting AIDS and other diseases through promiscuous sexual activity, more and more people
tolerate and even promote sex outside of marriage. Some of the
obvious, disheartening results of that trend are alarming increases
in illegitimate pregnancies and births (and as a result the steady
reliance on abortion to eliminate these "problems"), rapes and
child molestation, and a variety of venereal diseases. Even the
amount of pornographic and erotic content in movies and television, especially the various forms of sexual innuendo, has increased
startlingly during recent years.

I believe God's judgment is already on our society because of
such wicked attitudes and practices. Consider the number of
divorces, cases of domestic violence, dysfunctional families, and
murders and other violent crimes when sensual urges go uncon-
trolled. People cannot continue to violate God's standards of morality and integrity without eventually suffering some terrible
consequences.

When believers or professing believers are immoral, the immediate consequences are especially bad, because the testimony of the
Gospel and all true Christians is damaged. You may recall the negative impact of the evangelical scandals of the late 1980s or the cyn-
icism caused by news stories of priests' immorality with Catholic
youth.

Men and women engage in all sorts of illicit sex and perverse
behavior and are fully accepted by the world. But based on God's
standard, sexual impurity is always a sin and will always be
judged. The apostle Paul warned the Ephesian Christians:

Do not let immorality or any impurity or greed even be named among you, as is proper among saints.... For this you know with certainty, that no immoral or impure person or covetous man, who is an idolater, has an inheritance in the kingdom of Christ and God. Let no one deceive you with empty words, for because of these things the wrath of God comes upon the sons of disobedience.

—Eph. 5:3, 5-6

In 1 Corinthians 6:18 the apostle tells all believers to "flee immorality. Every other sin that a man commits is outside the body, but the immoral man sins against his own body."

The same basic Greek term is used for "immorality" in both those passages. The writer of Hebrews uses the same root word (*pornos*, from which we get *pornography*) for "fornicators" in Hebrews 13:4 as he admonishes, "Let marriage be held in honor among all, and let the marriage bed be undefiled; for fornicators and adulterers God will judge." The same sexual sin is condemned (implicitly or explicitly) in all three passages.

But God has provided the means for us to avoid such sexual sin through the institution of marriage. Paul says, "Because of immoralities, let each man have his own wife, and let each woman have her own husband" (1 Cor. 7:2).

However, the Lord did not establish marriage as a mere preventative against immorality. He views marriage as honorable and wants us to have the same high regard for it. We can do that in several ways. First, we honor marriage when the husband fulfills his duties as the head: "Christ is the head of every man, and the man is the head of a woman" (1 Cor. 11:3). Second, we honor marriage when wives submit to their husbands, as Sarah did to Abraham (1 Pet. 3:1, 6). Third, we honor marriage when we make sure it is regulated by mutual love and respect, as the apostle Peter instructs us: "You husbands likewise, live with your wives in an understanding way, as with a weaker vessel, since she is a woman; and grant her honor as a fellow-heir of the grace of life, so that your prayers may not be hindered" (1 Pet. 3:7). With the utmost sense of graciousness, love, and integrity, both husband and wife should have a selfless concern for the welfare of the other. Both should be focusing on what they can give rather than on what they can obtain.

God is serious about sexual purity. Sex is wonderful and fulfilling within marriage but harmful and destructive outside marriage. "For this is the will of God, your sanctification; that is, that you abstain from sexual immorality; that each of you know how to possess his own vessel in sanctification and honor" (1 Thess. 4:3-4). Part of our responsibility to morality and integrity of character is that we be sexually pure.

CONTENTMENT: BEING SATISFIED
WITH WHAT WE HAVE

Another aspect of personal holiness that is extremely important if we are to be people of complete integrity is contentment, or being satisfied with what God has given us. The author of Hebrews gives us this simple exhortation concerning contentment: "Let your way of life be free from the love of money, being content with what you have" (13:5).

Covetousness is one of the chief ways discontentment manifests itself. Covetousness is an attitude, a longing to acquire things. It means we set nearly all our attention and thought on gaining more money or having new possessions, whether we ever obtain them or not. An encounter early in the career of wealthy oil executive John D. Rockefeller (1839-1937) illustrates this attitude. A friend reportedly asked the young Rockefeller how much money he wanted. "A million dollars," he answered. After Rockefeller earned his first million dollars, his friend asked him how much more money he wanted. "Another million dollars," Rockefeller replied.

Rockefeller's desires further illustrate a law of diminishing returns with regard to covetousness: the more we get the more we want, and the more we want the less satisfied we are. The Preacher (probably Solomon, one who would understand this principle very well) wrote, "He who loves money will not be satisfied with money, nor he who loves abundance with its income. This too is vanity" (Eccles. 5:10).

According to Scripture, loving money is one of the most common ways we display covetousness. Money can be used to purchase almost all the other items we desire, and thus it is synonymous with lusting after material riches, whatever form they take. Obviously, we should seek to be free from any craving for material wealth. Such a desire indicates we are trusting in riches rather than in the living God. Paul told Timothy how he was to deal with this matter, and his command is especially applicable to Christians living in affluent Western cultures: "Instruct those who are rich in this present world not to be conceited or to fix their hope on the uncertainty of riches, but on God, who richly supplies us with all things to enjoy" (1 Tim. 6:17).

The Lord Jesus, in perhaps His most sobering parable, gives us a strong warning about the serious pitfalls related to covetousness and materialism:

> *"Beware, and be on your guard against every form of greed; for not even when one has an abundance does his life consist of his possessions." And He told them a parable, saying, "The land of a certain rich man was very productive. And he began reasoning to himself, saying, 'What shall I do, since I have no place to store my crops?' And he said, 'This is what I will do: I will tear down my barns and build larger ones, and there I will store all my grain and my goods. And I will say to my soul, "Soul, you have many goods laid up for many years to come; take your ease, eat, drink and be merry."' But God said to him, 'You fool! This very night your soul is required of you; and now who will own what you have prepared?' So is the man who lays up treasure for himself, and is not rich toward God."*
> —*Luke 12:15-21*

The love of money and material possessions is evidenced in a variety of ways. For some people, it remains just an attitude—they never acquire anything. But others do acquire wealth, and for them the thrill is in adding to what they have. They love to increase their bank accounts, build up their stock and investment portfolios, or become involved in new business ventures.

Some people love money just for its own sake and find satisfaction simply in hoarding what they have. Still others are conspicuous consumers who love to buy newer, more expensive things—nicer clothes, fancier home entertainment centers, better computers, more luxurious cars, bigger vacation homes—so they can flaunt their wealth. However the love of materialism shows itself, it displeases God. We are all tempted—some of us more times than others—to compromise our testimonies and forget our integrity for the sake of material gain. But God wants us to be content.

Scripture contains a number of practical guidelines by which we can enjoy the attitude of contentment. First, we must realize God's goodness and believe that as our Father, He will take care of us. The apostle Paul reminds us that "God causes all things to work together for good to those who love God, to those who are called according to His purpose" (Rom. 8:28).

Second, we should truly grasp the truth that God is omniscient. He knows our needs long before we ask Him to supply them. Jesus told the disciples, "Your Father knows that you need these things" (Luke 12:30).

The third vital ingredient for genuine contentment is that we consider what we deserve. We often have an inflated, self-important view of what we desire, and even more of what we need. But in reality, by the Lord's sovereign design, the smallest good thing we have is far more than we deserve. Like Jacob, we are "unworthy of all the lovingkindness and of all the faithfulness which Thou hast shown" (Gen. 32:10).

Fourth, God's Word exhorts us to recognize His sovereign supremacy. We will not be completely content until we see that His plan is not the same for all His children. What the Father lovingly gives to one believer, He just as lovingly withholds from another (cf. 1 Cor. 12:4-11). Hannah, Samuel's mother, spoke wisely and to the point concerning material blessings: "The LORD makes poor and rich" (1 Sam. 2:7). We might not be comfortable with the first part of that statement, but God knows that being rich is not necessarily the best plan for us. It could even be spiritually harmful for us (as it was for the rich man in Luke 12). The Lord provides us with just what we need and nothing less.

Finally, we must keep on reminding ourselves that worldly wealth and possessions are not the true riches. Our real treasure is in heaven. So Paul calls on us to set our minds "on the things above, not on the things that are on earth" (Col. 3:2). Ultimately, therefore, genuine contentment results from our communion with God the Father and with His Son. As we draw near to Christ, we are overwhelmed with the spiritual riches we have in Him, and material riches simply do not have the same perceived value they once had.

STEADFASTNESS: KEEPING PURE IN DOCTRINE

One of the Devil's more subtle tactics is to lead believers away from sound doctrine. If he can distract us with unscriptural, questionable, irrational, or shifting doctrines, Satan has rendered us for the most part ineffective. Even if we are not affected by any particular infiltration of false doctrine, our Christian walk can be greatly hampered by laziness, lack of vigilance, and simple ignorance regarding doctrinal basics. Bad doctrine or a weak understanding of sound doctrine makes us vulnerable to all sorts of bad practices, including a weak or non-existent standard of integrity. The author of Hebrews reminds us where our anchor is and again urges us along the right path: "Jesus Christ is the same yesterday and today, yes and forever. Do not be carried away by varied and strange teachings" (13:8-9).

False doctrine in various forms has plagued the church from the earliest days. False teachers weakened the early church, most notably the legalistic Judaizers in Galatia who distorted the Gospel. During the past 200 years theological liberalism and skepticism has undermined the church and caused many people to abandon essential doctrines such as the deity of Christ, the inspiration and authority of the Bible, and salvation by faith alone through grace alone. And as we noted in Chapter 2, today the professing evangelical church is weakened by many influences, from subjectivism, pragmatism, and psychotherapy, to a sloppy understanding of the Gospel and a misplaced sense of tolerance and ecumenism that wants to dilute and de-emphasize doctrine.

During his apostolic ministry, the encroachment of false doctrine into the lives of Christians in the new churches was Paul's greatest fear. He knew that doctrinal impurity was the underlying source for all kinds of ungodly behavior. Typical of Paul's fears was his deep concern for the Corinthians' spiritual welfare: "I am afraid, lest as the serpent deceived Eve by his craftiness, your minds should be led astray from the simplicity and purity of devotion to Christ" (2 Cor. 11:3).

Paul was also greatly exercised about the precarious status of believers in Galatia: "I am amazed that you are so quickly deserting Him who called you by the grace of Christ, for a different gospel; which is really not another; only there are some who are disturbing you, and want to distort the gospel of Christ" (Gal. 1:6-7). He realized that false teachers can be sincere, persuasive, believable, and even kind and likable. But Paul was also convinced that superficial, subjective measurements are not how we are to judge doctrine. The supreme standard is always the Word of God: "Even though we, or an angel from heaven, should preach to you a gospel contrary to that which we have preached to you [according to the Word], let him be accursed" (v. 8).

As we studied in Chapter 2, purity of doctrine is the crucial foundation upon which everything else in the Christian life rests. If we would be people who practice personal holiness and show forth true integrity, our doctrine must be sound.

In Romans 12:9 Paul presents us with three additional duties pertaining to personal holiness: "Let love be without hypocrisy. Abhor what is evil; cling to what is good." At first glance this threefold exhortation might appear somewhat more abstract than the commands we have just discussed from Hebrews 13. But I trust that as we look at Romans 12:9 you'll see how relevant its content is to Christian integrity. These admonitions further prove that the pursuit of holiness is not one that is mystical and undefined, but is practical and based on conscious obedience to God's Word.

LOVING WITHOUT HYPOCRISY

Agapē love is the greatest virtue of the Christian life. Yet that type of love was rare in pagan Greek literature. That's because the traits *agapē* portrays—unselfishness, self-giving, willful devotion, concern for the welfare of others—were mostly disdained in ancient Greek culture as signs of weakness.

However, the New Testament declares *agapē* to be the character trait around which all others revolve. The apostle John writes, "God is love, and the one who abides in love abides in God, and God abides in him" (1 John 4:16). Jesus Himself attaches great importance to love in His answer to the Jewish lawyer:

> *"Teacher, which is the great commandment in the Law?" And He said to him, "'You shall love the Lord your God with all your heart, and with all your soul, and with all your mind.' This is the great and foremost commandment. And the second is like it, 'You shall love your neighbor as yourself.' On these two commandments depend the whole Law and the Prophets."*
> *—Matt. 22:36-40; cf. Rom. 13:8, 10*

It therefore makes sense that the first "fruit of the Spirit is love" (Gal. 5:22), and that love for other believers is the primary way people will know that we are believers (John 13:35; cf. 1 Thess. 3:12; 1

John 3:18). The apostle Paul himself served fellow believers "in the Holy Spirit, in genuine love" (2 Cor. 6:6).

Agapē love is so much a part of personal holiness that John asserts, "We know that we have passed out of death into life, because we love the brethren. He who does not love abides in death" (1 John 3:14). A person who does not demonstrate real love in his life is not a believer. Without love we cannot presume to have eternal life, much less be a person of integrity.

HATING WHAT IS EVIL

It follows logically that the person who is seeking to demonstrate true *agapē* love will also hate evil. Hating evil is the flip side of having love, which, by definition, can't be attracted to or "rejoice in unrighteousness" (1 Cor. 13:6). Since "the fear of the Lord is the beginning of wisdom" (Prov. 9:10), it follows that "the fear of the Lord is to hate evil" (Prov. 8:13). The believer will "abhor what is evil" (Rom. 12:9) because that's what God does.

When we are faithful followers of Christ who seriously want to be known for our integrity, we cannot accommodate any form or degree of evil. But that is often easier said than accomplished. The fight to avoid evil is part of the larger battle for personal holiness. Even Paul confessed, "I am of flesh, sold into bondage to sin. For that which I am doing, I do not understand; for I am not practicing what I would like to do, but I am doing the very thing I hate. . . . For the good that I wish, I do not do; but I practice the very evil that I do not wish. But if I am doing the very thing I do not wish, I am no longer the one doing it, but sin which dwells in me. I find then the principle that evil is present in me, the one who wishes to do good. For I joyfully concur with the law of God in the inner man" (Rom. 7:14-15, 19-22). It might be a struggle, but when a believer confronts sin and sometimes succumbs to it, his inner, godly self will, with God's help, eventually disapprove and turn from the evil.

Conventional human wisdom says that the only way to hate evil is to be shocked by it. But the constant bombardment of our senses in today's multimedia culture, with all its immorality and violence, makes it hard to be shocked by anything. Sadly, many believers amuse themselves with larger and more continual doses of worldly and ungodly diversions. They rationalize their behavior by believing that because they are Christians, exposure to sin and evil will not have a lasting effect on them. But in reality, such constant intake makes Christians immune to the shocking nature of evil, which of course lessens their resistance to evil and makes them more accommodating.

If we truly hate evil, however, we will want simply to avoid it in the first place. Consider the godly man in Psalm 1: "How blessed is the man who does not walk in the counsel of the wicked, nor stand in the path of sinners, nor sit in the seat of scoffers! But his delight is in the law of the LORD, and in His law he meditates day and night" (vv. 1-2). We can't flirt with sin and evil and not be affected by them.

The apostle Paul, in both his letters to Timothy, says that the only safe response against the temptation of evil is to flee its attraction: "Flee from these things, you man of God; and pursue righteousness, godliness, faith, love, perseverance and gentleness" (1 Tim. 6:11). "Flee from youthful lusts, and pursue righteousness, faith, love and peace, with those who call on the Lord from a pure heart" (2 Tim. 2:22).

When we follow the Holy Spirit's leading and use His resources, we should be willing and able to resist evil no matter how frequently or intensely we are confronted by it. Because "we have the mind of Christ" (1 Cor. 2:16), we are able to "examine everything carefully; hold fast to that which is good; abstain from every form of evil" (1 Thess. 5:21-22).

HOLDING ON TO WHAT IS GOOD

Those verses in 1 Thessalonians 5 clearly call believers to be discerning, to evaluate everything carefully and thoughtfully. That's how we can judge, based on God's Word, what to reject and what to hold on to. It should be obvious that if we are to hate evil, we are to love and hold on to what is good.

In Romans 12:9 Paul says we are to "cling to what is good." The Greek word from which we derive "cling" strengthens the idea of holding on to something. The word (from the root for *glue*) came to be associated with any kind of physical, emotional, or spiritual bond. To become servants of Christ who walk with integrity, we must bind ourselves to everything that is inherently good, right, and worthy.

At the end of his exhortations to the Philippians, the apostle Paul provides us with a definition of "good" and a way to cling to it: "Finally, brethren, whatever is true, whatever is honorable, whatever is right, whatever is pure, whatever is lovely, whatever is of good repute, if there is any excellence and if anything worthy of praise, let your mind dwell on [or cling to] these things" (4:8). The key here is to separate ourselves from worldly things and saturate our minds with Scripture so that what is good rules in our lives and replaces what is evil (cf. Rom. 12:1-2).

We can't deny that the path to personal holiness requires disciplined effort and is often difficult. But along the way God provides us all the spiritual strength and scriptural resources we'll ever need to walk the path successfully. Our responsibility to strive for personal holiness, along with our obligation to give God the preeminence, is simply a step toward building a life without compromise. One final step is to be known as people of integrity among the people our lives touch. And that happens as we treat them according to God's standard.

THE OBLIGATIONS
OF PRACTICAL HOLINESS

Francis Schaeffer, one of the most influential Christian thinkers of the twentieth century, wrote the following paragraphs in the final chapter of his final book:

All men are our neighbors, and we are to love them as ourselves. We are to do this on the basis of creation, even if they are not redeemed, for all men have value because they are made in the image of God. Therefore they are to be loved even at great cost.

This is, of course, the whole point of Jesus' story of the good Samaritan: Because a man is a man, he is to be loved at all cost.

So, when Jesus gives the special command to love our Christian brothers, it does not negate the other command. The two are not antithetical. We are not to choose between loving all men as ourselves and loving the Christian in a special way. The two commands reinforce each other.

If Jesus has commanded so strongly that we love all men as our neighbors, then how important it is especially to love our fellow-Christians. If we are told to love all men as our neighbors—as ourselves—then surely, when it comes to those with whom we have the special bonds as fellow-Christians— having one Father through one Jesus Christ and being indwelt by one Spirit—we can understand how overwhelmingly important it is that all men be able to see an observable love for those with whom we have these special ties. Paul makes the double obligation clear in Galatians 6:10: "As we have therefore opportunity, let us do good unto all men, especially unto them who are of the household of faith." He does not negate the command to do good to all men. But it is still not meaningless to add, "especially unto them who are of the household of faith." This dual goal should be our Christian mentality, the set of our minds; we should be consciously thinking about it and what it means in our one-moment-at-a-time lives. It should be the attitude that governs our outward observable actions. (*The Great Evangelical Disaster* [Wheaton, Ill.: Crossway, 1984], 157-58; italics in original)

Dr. Schaeffer understood quite well the believer's responsibility toward other men. He saw the delicate balance we need to maintain between our special duty of loving fellow Christians (what he called "the mark of the Christian") and our more general duty to love unbelievers. Once we get a grasp of this concept and begin to live it out daily, people around us will be much more likely to sense that we are different. When they see that our love is genuine—that we have real integrity in our treatment of others—they may be led to inquire about our motivation and will thus hear the truth of the Gospel.

The whole matter of how we behave toward others involves what I call the obligation of practical holiness. Calling that responsibility an obligation may imply that it's difficult and burdensome. But it's not when our hearts are right—when we obey God and are committed to personal holiness. As we continue to pursue and understand what the Word says about our sanctification, our attitudes and actions toward those inside and outside the family of God will reflect Jesus Christ. When others, believers and unbelievers alike, can see Christ in us, we have developed a power only our Lord can give—a power that characterized Him as He dealt with people in this world—the power of integrity.

OUR RELATIONSHIP WITH OTHER BELIEVERS

The first phase of practical holiness—the one that must be our primary consideration—is how we interact with other Christians. Romans 12:10-13 is by no means exhaustive, but in it the apostle Paul gives us the essence of how we should behave toward other members of Christ's body: "Be devoted to one another in brotherly love; give preference to one another in honor; not lagging behind in diligence, fervent in spirit, serving the Lord; rejoicing in hope, persevering in tribulation, devoted to prayer, contributing to the needs of the saints, practicing hospitality."

Displaying Brotherly Love

Brotherly love is the key indicator by which the church proves to the world that it is genuine and belongs to Christ: "By this all men will know that you are My disciples, if you have love for one another" (John 13:35).

Such love is not only mandatory for Christians but inescapable, because "whoever loves the Father loves the child born of Him" (1 John 5:1). Earlier in his first letter, the apostle John made this point much more emphatically: "If someone says, 'I love God,' and hates his brother, he is a liar; for the one who does not love his brother whom he has seen, cannot love God whom he has not seen" (4:20). What utter hypocrisy is manifested by anyone who professes to be a Christian but does not love other believers!

The most elemental manifestation of brotherly love occurs when we care for fellow Christians more than we care for ourselves. Paul reminds us of the need to work toward this goal: "Do nothing from selfishness or empty conceit, but with humility of mind let each of you regard one another as more important than himself; do not merely look out for your own personal interests, but also for the interests of others" (Phil. 2:3-4).

A devotion to brotherly love should be an intuitive response by believers, especially those who are spiritually mature. That's why

Paul said to the Thessalonians, "As to the love of the brethren, you have no need for any one to write to you, for you yourselves are taught by God to love one another" (1 Thess. 4:9). The fact that God is our common heavenly Father should motivate us to love other Christians just as normally and naturally as we love other members of our biological family.

The kind of brotherly love Romans 12:10 refers to—"Be devoted to one another in brotherly love"—is not sentimental, superficial affection. Here and elsewhere in the New Testament it is based on deep and sincere concerns for the other person and results in practical commitment. "Whoever has the world's goods, and beholds his brother in need and closes his heart against him, how does the love of God abide in him?" (1 John 3:17). If love never results in practical application on behalf of fellow Christians, that calls into question the reality of your love for them and ultimately your love for God.

John goes on to urge us toward a consistent demonstration of true brotherly love: "Little children, let us not love with word or with tongue, but in deed and truth" (v. 18). The one who says he loves his brothers and sisters in Christ but doesn't prove it by his actions is a hypocrite. But the one who reveals the genuineness of his love by his actions has integrity.

Preferring One Another in Honor

Humility is a crucial aspect of brotherly love, so much so that it's almost assumed that those who truly love fellow believers will "give preference to one another in honor." The apostle Paul gave that command in Romans 12:10, but earlier in the chapter he had already spelled out the need for Christian humility: "For through the grace given to me I say to every man among you not to think more highly of himself than he ought to think; but to think so as to have sound judgment, as God has allotted to each a measure of faith" (v. 3; cf. Phil. 2:3).

The concept of giving honor in Romans 12:10 in no way means

you should flatter or lavish false praise on another. Rather, it means we are to show genuine thankfulness and respect for other members of God's family. Those who mouth empty compliments to gain a favor from someone betray their selfishness and lack of integrity. God wants us to be considerate of our brothers and sisters and quick to acknowledge their accomplishments.

Not Lagging Behind in Diligence

Since there is no room for sloth and indolence in the Lord's work, Paul exhorts us not to lag behind in diligence (Rom. 12:11). Solomon counsels us, "Whatever your hand finds to do, verily, do it with all your might; for there is no activity or planning or wisdom in Sheol [the grave]" (Eccles. 9:10). We need to make the most of whatever time the Lord has given us on earth. Many opportunities for Christian service come our way only once, and we must take advantage of them.

Carpe diem is a familiar Latin phrase that has become even more popular in recent years. It means, "Seize the day." That was Jesus' perspective His whole life. He told the disciples that He "must work the works of Him who sent Me, as long as it is day; night is coming, when no man can work" (John 9:4). Christ always sought to make the best, most effective use of His ministry because He knew the Father had allotted Him just so much time on earth to accomplish His will.

Lack of diligence in serving Christ not only wastes opportunities for good works, it also allows evil to prosper: "Therefore be careful how you walk, not as unwise men, but as wise, making the most of your time, because the days are evil" (Eph. 5:15-16). The writer of Proverbs 18 adds this warning: "He also who is slack in his work is brother to him who destroys" (v. 9). Laziness is analogous to the person who wishes to grow a bountiful vegetable garden but does not weed and tend it. It also brings to mind those property owners who neglect to mow their lawn or trim the trees and bushes around their homes (cf. Prov. 24:30-34).

All service for the Lord is worth doing with enthusiasm and care, and He will reward those who serve with such diligence. The author of Hebrews again has encouraging and instructive words:

> God is not unjust so as to forget your work and the love which you have shown toward His name, in having ministered and in still ministering to the saints. And we desire that each one of you show the same diligence so as to realize the full assurance of hope until the end, that you may not be sluggish, but imitators of those who through faith and patience inherit the promises.
>
> —Heb. 6:10-12

Being Fervent in Spirit

Henry Martyn, the faithful missionary to India in the early nineteenth century, used to say it was his heart's desire to "burn out for God." That's the attitude reflected in Paul's statement in Romans 12:11, which urges us to be "fervent in spirit."

The word for "fervent" in the Greek literally means "to boil." However, Paul's intention was to use the word metaphorically. Diligent believers ought to possess sufficient fervor to energize their work and ministry. But they are never to go to the extreme of becoming overheated and out of control, fanatically "boiling over" in their emotions.

Many failures, whether at home, in the workplace, or in ministry, are simply the result of indifference and lack of commitment. Believers often have good intentions, but when the zeal is absent, nothing will get done. But honest, full-fledged fervency requires resolve and persistence. Paul admonishes all of us who would be fervent in spirit, "Let us not lose heart in doing good, for in due time we shall reap if we do not grow weary" (Gal. 6:9).

The apostle himself was a model of that kind of fervency. He told the Corinthian church, "Therefore I run in such a way, as not without aim; I box in such a way, as not beating the air" (1 Cor. 9:26). And to the Colossians he said, "For this purpose also I labor" (Col. 1:29).

Serving the Lord

Fully committed, unequivocating service to God is the fifth aspect of behavior we are to exemplify before other Christians. "Serving the Lord" in Romans 12:11 calls us to examine our priorities. It also provides a focus for our diligence and fervency. First, everything we do must be consistent with Scripture; and, second, it should be something that is not detrimental to the cause of Christ but actually brings glory to His name. A stricter devotion to the Lord's standards helps us avoid or eliminate much fruitless activity in our personal lives and in our churches.

In verse 11 Paul uses the Greek word *douleō*, which means the service of a bond-slave. A bond-slave was the lowliest of servants, whose entire existence centered on doing his master's will. *Bond-slave* was the same term Paul chose on various occasions to describe his own relationship to Jesus Christ (e.g., Rom. 1:1; Phil. 1:1; Titus 1:1). The apostle always knew the importance of such a role: he was called to serve God and to preach the Gospel of Christ (cf. Rom. 1:9).

The Lord has called every believer to serve Him with a sense of priority and integrity. Yet we don't have to rely on our own strength to do so, any more than we drew upon our own power for salvation. We can be assured, along with Paul, that all the spiritual power we need to serve Christ also comes from Him: "For this purpose also I labor, striving according to His power, which mightily works within me" (Col. 1:29).

Rejoicing in Hope

Pursuing practical holiness and scriptural integrity will inevitably bring us a certain amount of opposition from the world, and at times even some resentment from fellow believers. We also may experience varying amounts of disappointment with ourselves. For example, after years of faithful and consistent service for the Lord, we might see little in the way of tangible fruit for our efforts.

Without the hope Paul mentions in Romans 12:12, we would never triumph over such obstacles.

The scriptural concept of hope is one in which we can have full confidence. In Romans 8:24-25 Paul says, "For in hope we have been saved, but hope that is seen is not hope; for why does one also hope for what he sees? But if we hope for what we do not see, with perseverance we wait eagerly for it" (cf. 1 Thess. 5:8; Heb. 6:17-19). Hope is not based on wishful thinking or mere probability; it is an integral aspect of our salvation. It also is certain: the Lord planned salvation before the foundation of the world, granted it to us in this present age, and promises to complete it in the future. Jesus assures us, "All that the Father gives Me shall come to Me; and the one who comes to Me I will certainly not cast out" (John 6:37).

God gives us many incentives to rejoice in hope, and therefore reasons to continue living righteously. He promises us in this present life that if we are "steadfast, immovable, always abounding in the work of the Lord," our "toil is not in vain" (1 Cor. 15:58). Regarding the future, God promises faithful believers that "there is laid up for [us] the crown of righteousness, which the Lord, the righteous Judge, will award to [us] on that day; and . . . to all who have loved His appearing" (2 Tim. 4:8; cf. Matt. 25:21).

Persevering in Tribulation

Such positive incentives and firm promises make it possible for us to be hopeful in all situations, even the most trying. When we possess integrity we will minister to fellow Christians, with their welfare as our goal, and as a result will be willing to persevere in tribulation (Romans 12:12), not be deterred by any obstacle, and endure any suffering. The apostle Paul highlights the benefits of this all-encompassing kind of perseverance: "We also exult in our tribulations, knowing that tribulation brings about perseverance; and perseverance, proven character; and proven character, hope; and hope does not disappoint, because the love of God has been poured out within our hearts through the Holy Spirit who was given to us" (Rom. 5:3-5).

Being Devoted to Prayer

One of the main reasons God challenges us with adversity is so we will learn to trust more fully in Him. And a key facet of relying on the Lord's strength rather than our own is being "devoted to prayer."

Paul uses the term "devoted" in Romans 12:12 to mean literally "strong toward something," in the sense of being steadfast and unwavering. The early Christians, even before the Holy Spirit descended on them at Pentecost, were strongly committed to the need for regular prayer: "These all with one mind were continually devoting themselves to prayer, along with the women, and Mary the mother of Jesus, and with His brothers" (Acts 1:14; cf. 2:42). The apostles also knew the importance of this principle and were determined to live by it. That's why they refused to let themselves be distracted by other demands. Instead, they directed the selection of the first deacons: "But select from among you, brethren, seven men of good reputation, full of the Spirit and of wisdom, whom we may put in charge of this task [serving food]. But we will devote ourselves to prayer, and to the ministry of the word" (Acts 6:3-4).

In developing practical holiness and integrity, we need to make earnest prayer as much a regular habit of our day as our other daily routines. If we are committed to such a discipline, we will pray "in the Holy Spirit" and "without ceasing" (Jude 20; 1 Thess. 5:17; cf. Eph. 6:18). That's why Paul instructed Timothy to have "the men in every place to pray, lifting up holy hands" (1 Tim. 2:8).

Contributing to the Needs of Other Believers

According to the laws of democratic, western cultures, people have the right to own certain basic things. But in God's eyes, no one owns anything—He owns it all. We are just stewards of the resources He has entrusted to us. One of the most important ways the Lord wants us to carry out our responsibilities as stewards is by "contributing to the needs of the saints" (Rom. 12:13), our brothers and sisters in Christ.

The word translated "contributing" in verse 13 is from the same Greek word we often use in its transliterated form, *koinonia*. It basically means to have something in common or in partnership, which involves mutual sharing and fellowship (see Acts 2:42, 44; 4:32). But here in the context of verse 13 the emphasis is on giving to others, hence the English rendering of "contributing." Paul used the same form with the same emphasis in 1 Timothy 6:17-18 when he told Timothy to "instruct those who are rich in this present world . . . to be generous and ready to share."

The believers in the various Macedonian churches Paul ministered to were eager to share in the offering he collected for the destitute Christians in Judea. The following passage from 2 Corinthians, describing the Macedonians' response to Paul's request for their participation in the offering, remains a classic admonition to us on what our own attitudes and actions should be when it comes to helping brothers and sisters in the church:

> *Now, brethren, we wish to make known to you the grace of God which has been given in the churches of Macedonia, that in a great ordeal of affliction their abundance of joy and their deep poverty overflowed in the wealth of their liberality. For I testify that according to their ability, and beyond their ability they gave of their own accord, begging us with much entreaty for the favor of participation in the support of the saints, and this, not as we had expected, but they first gave themselves to the Lord and to us by the will of God.*
> —8:1-5

Practicing Hospitality

Paul concludes his list of our duties to fellow believers by saying we have the responsibility of "practicing hospitality" toward others (Rom. 12:13), especially Christians. The phrase literally means "pursuing the love of strangers," which indicates we are not just to wait for emergencies or extraordinary situations to help someone. Instead, we are actually to look for opportunities in which we can show hospitality. The writer to the Hebrew Christians gives this additional admonition: "Do not neglect to show hospitality to strangers, for by this some have entertained angels without knowing it" (Heb. 13:2).

Hospitality is a biblical standard or qualification for elders in the local church (1 Tim. 3:2; Titus 1:8). Pastors and other church leaders should always be prepared to open their homes and serve the needs of others. Genuine hospitality will also be the mark of spiritually mature women in the church (1 Tim. 5:10). All believers should be known as people who practice hospitality. It is an essential quality of Christian integrity, not some incidental or optional activity.

The second half of Hebrews 13:2, "some have entertained angels without knowing it," is regularly cited as our motivation for displaying hospitality. But that is not an accurate understanding or application of the phrase. We are not to be hospitable to our brethren or strangers simply because we think we might someday encounter individuals who are supernatural messengers from God. The real point is that we can never know all the ramifications of a simple act of loving helpfulness. The Lord wants us to minister because we realize it's the right thing to do and because there's a need.

In Genesis 18 Abraham viewed his chance to help the three men as an opportunity, not as a way to impress some travelers who might be angels. In fact he felt humble and privileged that they would even accept his hospitality: "My lord, if now I have found favor in your sight, please do not pass your servant by" (v. 3). At first Abraham did not know that the three men were special, yet he still volunteered to help them.

Jesus reminds us that we always minister to Him when we are hospitable, especially to His servants: "Truly I say to you, to the extent that you did it to one of these brothers of Mine, even the least of them, you did it to Me" (Matt. 25:40). If we turn our backs on those who need food, who need a place to stay, who need clothing, who need to be visited in prison or the hospital, we are actually turning our backs on Christ (v. 45).

OUR RELATIONSHIP WITH STRANGERS AND ALL PEOPLE

The virtue of ministering to strangers forms a transitional link between our relationship to fellow believers and our relationship to all other people. That's because when we reach out with an act of kindness or service to a stranger, the person could be either a believer or an unbeliever. Both the author of Hebrews and the apostle Paul give us specific exhortations concerning our duty toward those we don't know. Let's begin by continuing our look at Paul's list of practical holiness traits in Romans 12:14-16.

Blessing Those Who Persecute Us

"Bless those who persecute you; bless and curse not" (Rom. 12:14) is one of the most difficult of all the exhortations to us concerning practical holiness. It goes so much against the grain of our human feelings and logic, yet Paul urges us to obey it. And that was simply in keeping with Jesus' original instructions: "I say to you who hear, love your enemies, do good to those who hate you, bless those who curse you, pray for those who mistreat you" (Luke 6:27-28; cf. Matt. 5:44).

Lest we be tempted to think Jesus' words are impractical and merely idealistic, He gives some specific examples of how we are to treat people who mistreat us: "Whoever hits you on the cheek, offer him the other also; and whoever takes away your coat, do not withhold your shirt from him either. Give to everyone who asks of you, and whoever takes away what is yours, do not demand it back" (Luke 6:29-30).

Furthermore, Christ expects us to treat our persecutors as our friends. He told the disciples, "If you love those who love you, what credit is that to you? For even sinners love those who love them. And if you do good to those who do good to you, what credit is that to you? For even sinners do the same thing" (vv. 32-33).

Jesus Himself is the ultimate example of one who blessed His persecutors. While He hung on the cross, He prayed that most merciful of prayers for those who wanted Him killed: "Father, forgive them; for they do not know what they are doing" (Luke 23:34). The apostle Peter reminds us of the Savior's example and tells we must adopt the same attitude when we face persecution: "For you have been called for this purpose, since Christ also suffered for you, leaving you an example for you to follow in His steps, who committed no sin, nor was any deceit found in His mouth; and while being reviled, He did not revile in return; while suffering, He uttered no threats, but kept entrusting Himself to Him who judges righteously" (1 Peter 2:21-23).

Learning to Sympathize and Empathize

Hebrews 13:3 urges us to identify with all those in need, and to do our best, with the Spirit's help, to put ourselves in their places: "Remember the prisoners, as though in prison with them, and those who are ill-treated, since you yourselves also are in the body." The point is, we should do for other people as we would want them to do for us, which is just a reiteration of Jesus' golden rule: "Therefore whatever you want others to do for you, do so for them, for this is the Law and the Prophets" (Matt. 7:12).

Under divine inspiration, the author of Hebrews brings us into the practical realm as we seek to have integrity in all our dealings with people. His words provide a balance against the tendencies we sometimes have to spiritualize the truth and deny the realities of pain, struggle, and hardships in life. Our own difficulties should never be an excuse for not ministering to others. Instead, they should be incentives and tools for us to be more understanding and helpful to others.

There are at least five significant and practical ways we can sympathize and empathize with others. First, we can simply be available when others need us. There are times when that does more to encourage and strengthen our friends than any kind words and good deeds can.

Second, we can give direct help to someone. The parable of the Good Samaritan (Luke 10:30-37) comes immediately to mind as a prime example of meeting someone's physical needs by taking direct responsibility for that person's welfare. The Philippians' monetary gift greatly helped Paul extend his ministry in Asia Minor. Their sharing was also a great spiritual encouragement to him: "You have done well to share with me in my affliction" (Phil. 4:14).

A third way to show empathy and sympathy is through prayer. Paul sought prayer from the brothers and sisters in the church at Thessalonica (1 Thess 5:25; 2 Thess. 3:1), but he also was faithful to pray for them: "To this end also we pray for you always that our God may count you worthy of your calling, and fulfill every desire for goodness and the work of faith with power" (2 Thess. 1:11).

The apostle's parting words to the Colossians included a further request for prayer: "Remember my imprisonment" (Col. 4:18). They couldn't visit Paul, and money would not have helped. But he knew that prayer was a powerful way the Colossian believers could support him.

Romans 12:15 gives us two additional principles for identifying with the ups and downs in other people's lives: "Rejoice with those who rejoice, and weep with those who weep."

On the surface, rejoicing with others who rejoice would seem easy enough. However, the temptation to engage in jealousy and resentment is often present when we hear about someone else's good news. Their happiness and success could be at our expense, or their special circumstances make ours pale by comparison. But God calls us to demonstrate joy when things go well for others—especially other Christians—no matter how badly we might want to make unfavorable comparisons to our own circumstances.

As always, the apostle Paul set the standard and practiced what he taught. He instructed the Corinthians, "If one member is honored, all the members rejoice with [him or her]" (1 Cor. 12:26). Later he assured them, "My joy would be the joy of you all" (2 Cor. 2:3).

Finally, to develop sympathy and empathy for others we must sometimes "weep with those who weep." Compassion in a believer is critical because it reflects our Lord's attitude. We must be ready to enter into the pain, suffering, disappointment, and various setbacks that others experience. The Lord is so compassionate toward us, His people, that Jeremiah the prophet rightly asserts, "His compassions never fail" (Lam. 3:22). God displayed his tenderheartedness practically when His Son, the Lord Jesus, wept because His friend Lazarus was dead (John 11:35). And on that occasion Jesus also showed great sympathy to Lazarus' sisters, Mary and Martha. If we want to be more conformed to the image of Christ, sometimes we'll have to identify with the sorrows of others.

In summary Paul says, "As those who have been chosen of God, holy and beloved, put on a heart of compassion, kindness, humility, gentleness and patience" (Col. 3:12). Bearing each other's burdens through sympathy and empathy fulfills the law of Christ (Gal. 6:2), which is love. Again Jesus is our unsurpassed role model: "We do not have a high priest who cannot sympathize with our weaknesses" (Heb. 4:15). Therefore, we have no excuse or reason not to sympathize with others, particularly believers, who have need.

Being Impartial

Romans 12:16 opens with the command to "be of the same mind toward one another." Several chapters later, as if to underscore the importance of the words, Paul repeats the phrase: "Now may the God who gives perseverance and encouragement grant you to be of the same mind with one another according to Christ Jesus" (15:5). The apostle is urging us to have impartiality in all our dealings with others, and especially with those in the church.

The clearest New Testament warning against partiality is from the pen of the apostle James:

My brethren, do not hold your faith in our glorious Lord Jesus Christ with an attitude of personal favoritism. For if a man comes into your assembly with a gold ring and dressed in fine clothes, and there also comes in a poor man in dirty clothes, and you pay special attention to the one who is wearing the fine clothes, and say, "You sit here in a good place," and you say to the poor man, "You stand over there, or sit down by my footstool," have you not made distinctions among yourselves, and become judges with evil motives? . . . But if you show partiality, you are committing sin and are convicted by the law as transgressors.

—James 2:1-4, 9; cf. 1 Tim. 5:21

The principle of practical holiness could hardly be stated and illustrated any more effectively. If we serve an impartial God (Rom. 2:11; cf. Acts 10:34; 1 Peter 1:17), it is imperative that we minister to others impartially and with complete integrity.

Avoiding Elitism

Paul continues in Romans 12:16 with a caution that is closely related to the exhortation to be impartial: "Do not be haughty in mind, but associate with the lowly." He in essence instructs us to guard against any temptation to be elitist or to pursue a self-centered, high-minded pride. (Not to be "haughty in mind" literally means not to be "minding high things.")

If partiality leads to a condescending lack of respect and an aversion to the poor, as the James 2 passage teaches, then it is not surprising that the apostle Paul would tell us to "associate with the lowly." The point is not that we should necessarily stop having any interaction with wealthy or influential persons. But we should consider and act on the greater obligation we have to the poor, simply because they are much more in need.

There is no place for an aristocracy or an elite upper crust in the church. When such an attitude exists, the integrity of the ministry suffers. Our Lord Jesus, in a descriptive and convicting illustration, makes the point extremely well about our duty to associate with and meet the needs of the lowliest, most disadvantaged people. In the following illustration, Christ is not condemning inviting family, friends, or wealthy people to our homes. He is, however, revealing the sinfulness of our wrong, self-serving motives in inviting only people who can repay us:

"When you give a luncheon or a dinner, do not invite your friends or your brothers or your relatives or rich neighbors, lest they also invite you in return, and repayment come to you. But when you give a reception, invite the poor, the crippled, the lame, the blind, and you will be blessed, since they do not have the means to repay you; for you will be repaid at the resurrection of the righteous."

—Luke 14:12-14

Avoiding Conceit

The very notion of a conceited Christian who relies solely on his own wisdom is inconsistent with who he is. Just as there is no room in the church for social elitism, neither is there a place for intellectual elitism. In the final phrase of Romans 12:16 the apostle Paul gives all believers the straightforward command, "Do not be wise in your own estimation." This concept is not limited to Paul's correspondence with the Romans (cf. Phil. 2:3), nor is it even limited to the New Testament. The writer of Proverbs 3, probably Solomon, says, "Do not be wise in your own eyes" (v. 7). The warning against conceit is a well-established scriptural principle that we must not ignore.

To underscore the importance of this principle even more, consider the apostle Paul's classic discourse on man's wisdom versus God's wisdom:

For consider your calling, brethren, that there were not many wise according to the flesh, not many mighty, not many noble; but God has chosen the foolish things of the world to shame the wise, and God has chosen the weak things of the world to shame the things which are strong, and the base things of the world and the despised, God has chosen, the things that are not, that He might nullify the things that are, that no man should boast before God. But by His doing you are in Christ Jesus, who became to us wisdom from God, and righteousness and sanctification, and redemption, that, just as it is written, "Let him who boasts, boast in the Lord."

—*1 Cor. 1:26-31*

When we seek to serve Christ faithfully, practice holiness, and live with integrity, we will humbly submit to the will of God found in His Word. Our ultimate confidence cannot exist in ourselves or in our own wisdom and talents, but only in Him.

OUR RELATIONSHIP WITH OUR PERSONAL ENEMIES

As we have already noted, one of the most difficult and challenging aspects in the pursuit of practical holiness is, How do we behave toward those who persecute us (Rom. 12:14)? To treat our persecutors as our friends and to bless them definitely cuts across the grain of our unredeemed flesh. We certainly need as much divine assistance and scriptural instruction as possible when it comes to relating to our opponents. Therefore in Romans 12:17-21 the apostle Paul returns to the theme of verse 14 and elaborates on it.

Not Returning Evil for Evil

Paul first admonishes us to "never pay back evil for evil to anyone" (v. 17). Here Paul seeks to clarify the misunderstanding we could have of the Old Testament law that said, "But if there is any further injury, then you shall appoint as a penalty life for life, eye for eye, tooth for tooth, hand for hand, foot for foot, burn for burn, wound for wound, bruise for bruise" (Ex. 21:23-25).

Those verses in Exodus 21 pertained to civil justice in Israel and are not to be applied to personal vengeance. Actually, the main purpose of such laws was to make sure the punishment was proportional to the crime. For example, someone found guilty of putting out somebody else's eye could suffer the forfeiture of his own eye, but nothing more.

Personal grievances, even the most horrible wrongs, are not to be settled by vengeance. As people who would obey Christ in all things, we must not take the law into our own hands and seek justice by whatever means is most expedient or personally satisfying. Even the majority of secular society still strongly disapproves of a vigilante mentality. Matters of legal justice must be left in the hands of God-ordained civil authorities (cf. Rom. 13:1-7).

The apostle Peter, in his first letter, reinforces for us the truth of Paul's admonitions about paying back evil: "To sum up, let all be harmonious, sympathetic, brotherly, kindhearted, and humble in spirit; not returning evil for evil, or insult for insult, but giving a blessing instead; for you were called for the very purpose that you might inherit a blessing" (3:8-9).

Respecting What Is Right

In the second half of Romans 12:17, Paul arms us with a powerful antidote against the temptation to angrily repay evil for evil. He urges us to "respect what is right in the sight of all men." If we honestly do that, we will develop, with God's help, a right attitude toward those who oppose us.

Such an attitude of respect prepares us ahead of time to respond to evil with what is good rather than with what is bad. The goodness the Lord would expect us to express in those situations is not to be passive and internal but active and external, so that others may see it. In that way our gracious behavior toward our enemies should be a positive testimony to them and "adorn the doctrine of God our Savior in every respect" (Titus 2:10).

Living at Peace with Everyone

A peaceful relationship, by definition, cannot be one-sided. Therefore, this characteristic of our relationship with our enemies will not always occur. Just by examining what the apostle Paul writes in Romans 12:18—"If possible, so far as it depends on you, be at peace with all men"—we can determine that living at peace with others is a conditional command. At least half the success is dependent on the attitudes and responses of the other person.

However, the conditional nature of Paul's admonition concerning peaceful relations does not mean it's optional. Any believer who wants to live in integrity has no excuse regarding his responsibility to pursue peace in every relationship. The Lord wants us to have an inner desire to sincerely live peacefully with all varieties of people, even the most unlovable, the most inconsiderate, the most hostile, or the most obnoxious.

As long as we don't compromise the scriptural limitations on our relationships with unbelievers, God wants us to be willing to bend over backwards to build peaceful bridges to any persons who hate us and persecute us. That means we cannot hold a grudge or harbor bitterness toward them. We must instead extend genuine, heartfelt forgiveness. Then we can honestly begin the process of seeking reconciliation, the results of which are in God's hands.

Overcoming Evil with Good

The apostle Paul concludes the passage in Romans 12 about the Christian's relationship to his enemies by quoting the centuries-old injunction "But if your enemy is hungry, feed him, and if he is thirsty, give him a drink; for in so doing you will heap burning coals upon his head" (v. 20; cf. Prov. 25:21-22). After again denouncing the sin of personal vengeance (Rom. 12:19), Paul uses the Old

Testament to confront us with the more difficult, positive aspect of dealing with evil. To avoid taking revenge against another, all we have to do is do nothing. But it is much more challenging to go beyond that passive response and repay an evil deed with a good deed.

The notion of placing burning coals on someone's head refers to an ancient Egyptian custom. Someone who wanted to show his contrition publicly would carry a pan of burning coals on his head. Such symbolism represented an admission of pain, guilt, and shame. In a modern context, if we lovingly meet someone's needs and are kind to him even though he has sinned against us, we shame him for his evil behavior.

Paul summarizes his teaching on our relationship to our enemies by urging us not to let evil defeat us: "Do not be overcome by evil, but overcome evil with good" (v. 21). That means none of the evil done to us by other people should overwhelm us. And even more important, our own evil responses should never overcome us.

Neither one of those fates will befall us, however, if we keep our priorities straight. And our priorities will be in order if we simply rely on God's power to help us carry out the duties of practical holiness, the Scripture-based attitudes and actions we have discussed in this chapter. If we focus our energies in those directions, we won't have time to be intimidated and overpowered by the negative things others might hurl at us. At the same time, we will be so Spirit-controlled that our own fleshly tendencies will not consume us and control how we relate to those who oppose us. As the apostle Paul says in Romans 12:21, the key in all such situations is to "overcome evil with good."

That's a fitting conclusion to our look at the power of integrity because it summarizes the outlook we must maintain at all times. We live in an evil world, and the only true good in it is what God brings into it. And He accomplishes that primarily through our faithful obedience to Him.

The power of integrity is simple really: obey God and watch Him use you to transform lives around you. The opposite of obedience is compromise, and no one will be particularly impressed with that because it is so characteristic of people today. You need to stand out and be counted among those who name Jesus Christ as their Lord and Savior. When you do, you will fulfill the verses we highlighted at the beginning of this book: "O LORD, who may abide in Thy tent? Who may dwell on Thy holy hill? He who walks with integrity, and works righteousness, and speaks truth in his heart" (Ps. 15:1-2).

STUDY GUIDE

CHAPTER 1:
VALUE UNSURPASSED

Summarizing the Chapter

The heart and soul of Christianity is the believer's relationship with Christ. As such, it is the necessary starting point for building a life of integrity.

Getting Started (Choose One)

1. Make a list of all the things you truly value. What would you take, for example, if you knew a fast-approaching tornado would likely level your home? Now divide your list into two categories: material possessions and personal relationships. Which category outweighs the other?

2. If you replace a dying tree or shrub in your yard with a new one, what would you typically do with the old plant? Would there ever be a legitimate reason for grafting any of the old branches onto the new tree?

Answering the Questions

1. What is the heart and soul of all Christianity? Explain.

2. Before he met Christ on the road to Damascus, what did Paul value and why? What did Paul come to realize about those things after he met Christ?

3. Explain the transaction that occurs when a person is saved. What happens to the believer's old nature?

4. What changes should occur in a person's lifestyle after he becomes a Christian? Why?

5. What effect does a person's salvation have on his mind?

6. Explain what "knowing" Christ means.

7. What is the greatest of all benefits each believer receives when he or she is saved? Explain.

8. Explain how knowledge of Christ's resurrection helps Christians in their daily battle with sin.

9. In what ways are suffering and persecution beneficial to Christians?

Focusing on Prayer

- Ask God to impress on you those areas of your relationship with Christ in which you need to improve. As He does so, ask Him for guidance on how you might specifically begin to apply the appropriate spiritual truths each day.

- Ask the Lord to reveal to you the ways in which you tend to follow the world's priorities and compromise His truth. As He does this, pray for guidance on how you can reverse those trends.

Applying the Truth

Read and study Colossians 3:1-17. Make a list of every word or phrase that refers to transformation or renewal. Next to each one, write what kind of behavior ought to result from that transformation. Begin to set goals and objectives for accomplishing those behavior patterns so that you will better reflect your commitment to Christ.

CHAPTER 2:

DOCTRINAL INTEGRITY

Summarizing the Chapter

Next to our relationship to Christ, the greatest source for living with integrity is a sincere commitment to God's Word as the final authority for truth and conduct.

Getting Started (Choose One)

1. Most of you have no doubt purchased or received as a gift an item that required some assembly. How did you approach the task? Did you dive right in without following the instructions, give the directions a quick read and then start assembling, or follow the instructions carefully as you put together each specific part? How easy or difficult was the process?

2. Many things in this world are available for the right price. How much would you be willing to pay, for example, to purchase the car of your dreams? How much would you pay to travel to your favorite place in the world? How much would you pay for the home of your dreams? How much would you be willing to pay to protect God's Word from those who would compromise it? Would you protect His Word at the expense of your life?

Answering the Questions

1. What ultimately leads Christians to compromise God's standard?

2. What are some of the ways in which God's Word is compromised in the church today?

3. Why is the leadership in many churches dominated by immature Christians?

4. What is the ultimate basis for unity in the church? In what ways has unity been compromised in Christianity today?

5. What is the church's mission in the world? Explain.

6. How can each Christian safeguard God's Word from those who would compromise its truths?

7. What is the central truth of God's Word that all believers must proclaim?

8. Explain how the Holy Spirit uses the Gospel to reach those God has chosen for salvation.

9. What should characterize all those who seek to become leaders in the church?

10. What must exist in every believer before he can live the Christian life effectively?

Focusing on Prayer

- Ask God to direct you to one or more people to whom you can proclaim the Gospel. Ask Him to give you boldness yet humility in your presentation, knowing that He alone can give them the gift of salvation.

- Pray for your church and your leaders. They have a great responsibility before God, and one of those is to be true and loyal to His Word. Ask God to help them be constantly nourished on His Word and to remain committed to live out its truth moment by moment and day by day.

Applying the Truth

Review the list of activities that every Christian should be doing to safeguard God's truth. Each day take one of those duties and determine what you can do to make that responsibility a reality in your life. Begin to incorporate each duty into your life until it becomes a good habit.

CHAPTER 3:

IN PURSUIT OF GODLINESS

Summarizing the Chapter

The third necessary component for a life of integrity is a desire for godliness, which will bear God-honoring spiritual fruit in the life of the Christian.

Getting Started (Choose One)

1. How much emphasis does your employer place on you for job improvement? Does your employer's attitude fit in with your own plans for career progress? Why or why not?

2. We've all seen a decline in the commitment to excellence in today's world. Briefly relate an experience that underscored that fact vividly for you. What missing virtue could have made a positive difference in the situation?

Answering the Questions

1. What happened at the end of Jesus' earthly ministry that should encourage us every day to live godly lives (see Rom. 7:4)?

2. What other two traits did the apostle Paul sometimes group with love? Which of the three did he rate as superior?

3. How is the world's primary criterion for love most different from the decisive love (*agapē*) Paul prayed for?

4. How and on what occasion did Jesus best demonstrate a dynamic love toward His disciples?

5. If we "approve the things that are excellent," what one-word quality are we displaying? What choices does this quality encompass?

6. What's a good, concise definition of *spiritual integrity*? How can this concept be illustrated?

7. What was the "sunlight test"? How does it relate to the pursuit of godliness?

8. What are the two basic varieties of New Testament good works?

9. What practical character trait is necessary if we wish to abide in Christ and consistently obey His Word? How will others know if we have this trait?

Focusing on Prayer

• Pray that the quality of love in your life would be more and more as God wants it, and less and less as the world exhibits it.

• Ask the Lord to make you a thinking Christian, one who can discern between the good and the best. Pray for a specific issue in which you need guidance and wisdom to choose the best option.

Applying the Truth

Read, study, and meditate on John 13:3-17. Take special notice of the contrast between Christ's attitude and Peter's. Ask the Lord to give you an opportunity within the next month to lovingly reach out and help someone with a specific need. Be alert for the needs of those in your church, but don't overlook ways you might help neighbors or coworkers.

CHAPTER 4:

THE CONSEQUENCES OF AN UNCOMPROMISING LIFE

Summarizing the Chapter

Daniel's uncompromising lifestyle is an excellent and unmistakable example of what it means to live with integrity.

Getting Started (Choose One)

1. Name a contemporary person who has been a great inspiration to you regarding integrity. Explain briefly why you picked him or her. (The person may be someone you know personally or someone the rest of the group would also recognize.)

2. Today's culture seems to make it more and more difficult for us to know where to draw the line regarding certain beliefs and practices. Talk about one such consideration that presents a special challenge for you.

Answering the Questions

1. What personal qualities does the world look for when filling important leadership positions (see Dan. 1:3-4)?

2. How did the term *Chaldean* become synonymous with *Babylonian*?

3. What ultimate goal did the Babylonians have in mind for Daniel's reeducation program?

4. List some other major Bible characters who displayed unashamed boldness in trusting the Lord.

5. How did God establish a higher standard for the priesthood (Lev. 10:8-11)? Does this have any application for church leaders today?

6. When and how did Paul exemplify Daniel's kind of perseverance (see especially Acts 20:24; 21:10-14)?

7. What essential standards will an unblemished faith uphold? What is the source for these standards?

Focusing on Prayer

- Review the five characteristics of integrity from this chapter, and ask God to strengthen the ones that are weak in your life.

- Ask God to help you use Scripture as you draw the line concerning your convictions. Spend some extra time in prayer if you are facing an issue that is testing your determination to remain uncompromised.

Applying the Truth

Read the entire book of Daniel during the next two weeks. Take notes each day, and write out specific verses as additional things impress you about Daniel's wisdom and integrity. (One passage to devote extra study and meditation to would be Daniel's prayer in 9:4-19.)

CHAPTER 5:
FIRE AND LIONS

Summarizing the Chapter

Accompanied by the vicious opposition of worldly opponents, the fiery furnace and the lions' den tested but failed to mar the integrity of Daniel and his three friends.

Getting Started (Choose One)

1. Discuss your thoughts about the wisdom of holding a personal conviction on something Scripture is not dogmatic about. If you've ever tried to adhere to such a principle, was it as successful as Hudson Taylor's experience?

2. Peer pressure can be a difficult thing to deal with. How much of a problem, if any, is this for you at home, at work, at school? How are you coping with it?

Answering the Questions

1. What motivated Nebuchadnezzar to build the huge statue in Daniel 2?

2. Why did the lower-ranking officials initially resent Daniel's three friends? What intensified their resentment?

3. What was the uncommonly high standard that allowed Shadrach, Meshach, and Abed-nego to resist following the crowd?

4. How did the three men's behavior affect the king?

5. What two things concerning Daniel does the expression "extraordinary spirit" indicate?

6. Why did Daniel's opponents have to resort to creative scheming if they were going to trip him up?

7. What effect did Daniel's lifestyle have on King Darius' words and actions?

Focusing on Prayer

- Pray for missionary efforts in areas (for example, Islamic countries) where the culture is especially resistant to the Gospel. If you know a specific missionary who might be facing persecution, pray for that person.

- Ask God to help you be diligent and honest in all you do and to avoid the temptation to take shortcuts.

Applying the Truth

Memorize Psalm 18:22-23 or 84:11-12, and look for an opportunity to share it with someone in the next month.

CHAPTER 6:
IN DEFENSE OF INTEGRITY

Summarizing the Chapter

Paul was a role model of trustworthy and consistent integrity. When obliged to defend his integrity against false attacks, he did so with clarity, earnestness, and humility.

Getting Started (Choose One)

1. As this chapter shows, our faith is the most important thing in life worth defending. Name several other areas that the world sees as important. From your experience, what's the one thing people hold in highest esteem for their lives? Why?

2. Do you regularly set self-improvement goals or achievement goals? Why or why not? What have you found most helpful as a motivational device in helping you reach such goals?

Answering the Questions

1. What basic issues were involved in the Downgrade Controversy, which occurred during Charles Spurgeon's time?

2. What general things did Paul's opponents accuse him of? What was their motivation?

3. Paul had many reasons for having to defend his integrity, but what was the primary issue (see 2 Cor. 4:7)?

4. What is a synonym for fear, as in "the fear of God"? Cite one Bible reference to illustrate this.

5. What prudent approach did Paul choose in dealing with the various personal criticisms hurled at him by his enemies?

6. What does the phrase "beside ourselves" mean in 2 Corinthians 5:13? Why is it so important to interpret it precisely?

7. What is the overriding reason Paul had for feeling such gratitude for Christ's love? How should this reason affect all believers? Explain.

8. What passage perhaps best spells out the intensity of Paul's burden for the lost?

9. What is a good, one-sentence definition of *humility*?

10. Why was Paul able to be content to minister within certain boundaries? Give several reasons.

11. What did the false teachers attempt to take credit for in the church at Corinth?

12. What are two of the most common human standards by which people attempt to measure God's blessing of their ministry?

Focusing on Prayer

- Pray that the Lord would give you a daily hunger for His truth and His righteousness.

- Examine the areas in your life where you might be too proud. Pray that God and His Word would show you ways to be more humble.

Applying the Truth

Write out 2 Corinthians 4:7 or Micah 6:8 on an index card and place it where you will see it frequently during the next week. Let the verse be a reminder to you at those times when pride taints your words, actions, and attitudes. Do this long enough so you can keep track of your growth in humility; record times you did and did not remember your verse when tested by pride. Assess your progress after several months.

CHAPTER 7:

WITH FEAR AND TREMBLING:

THE ANTIDOTE TO HYPOCRISY

Summarizing the Chapter

The ideal scriptural remedy for hypocrisy occurs when we diligently pursue sanctification, realizing at the same time our complete dependence on God for the results.

Getting Started (Choose One)

1. In your view, what is the most frequent way people show hypocrisy in everyday living? What have you found as the best method for coping with such behavior?

2. Up to this point in your Christian experience, which approach to personal sanctification have you been taught the most? Have you tried to apply that teaching? How has it worked?

Answering the Questions

1. What is the original definition of *hypocrite*?

2. Has hypocrisy been particularly prevalent during a certain period in the Bible or church history?

STUDY GUIDE

3. Name at least three Scripture passages that deal with the subject of hypocrisy.

4. What is the basic emphasis of quietism? What verse is often used to support this view?

5. What does pietism advocate? How can that be harmful to our walk with Christ?

6. What insight does the ancient writer Strabo provide us in understanding the expression "work out" in Philippians 2:12?

7. Explain briefly the proper interpretation of the phrase "with fear and trembling."

8. What two divinely-produced attitudes should help move our wills toward holiness?

9. According to Philippians 2:13, why should we as Christians be motivated to do good works? What is another meaning of "pleasure" in this verse?

10. What remaining ingredient is necessary for us to succeed in the process of sanctification (1 Cor. 9:25-27)?

Focusing on Prayer

- Prayerfully examine your heart in the coming days, and ask the Lord to show you any areas of your life in which you've regularly behaved hypocritically. Repent of those actions, and ask God to help you be more faithful. If no problems are brought to mind, thank Him for His faithful mercies toward you.

- Ask God to give you a more balanced Christian life, based on the truth of Philippians 2:12-13.

Applying the Truth

Make some time for extended prayer, and pray through 1 Kings 8:56-61. Take long enough to pray over each verse and important thought.

Write down items the Lord impresses on your heart that you can do to conform better to the desires of Solomon's words (for example, a bad habit to forsake, a way to be more diligent in Bible study, etc.).

CHAPTER 8:

RENDER UNTO GOD

Summarizing the Chapter

If we continually put God first and seek to obey several principles from Hebrews 13:10-21, we will be people who live without compromise in a busy world.

Getting Started (Choose One)

1. Imagine if for one day, or even one week, you could not use a daily planner or calendar. How would that affect your use of time and the control of your priorities? Do you think you would get as much done as normal?

2. Is your supervisor at work easy or difficult to get along with and work for? Briefly share an experience that made it challenging for you to be submissive to him or her. How did you resolve the situation?

Answering the Questions

1. What story in Luke 10:38-42 illustrates the difficulty believers can have in seeking God first?

2. What does Hebrews 13:13 mean when it says Jesus "suffered outside the gate"?

3. If properly understood, how does separation from the world affect our relationship with unbelievers?

4. What attitude should continually accompany our actions of sacrificial living? What three verses from Psalms illustrate that?

5. What three categories of persons are we commanded to serve and obey submissively?

6. What challenge do spiritual leaders experience more intensely than the average Christian, and what should that urge us to do?

Focusing on Prayer

• Ask God to keep you mindful each day that He is to be first in your life.

• Pray that you will more successfully separate yourself from worldly temptations and sins that threaten your life of integrity.

Applying the Truth

Write a note of encouragement and appreciation to one of your local, state, or national officials, and tell that individual you are supporting him or her with prayer. You might want to include some appropriate verses of Scripture or a short piece of Christian literature (a tract or booklet).

CHAPTER 9:

THE RESPONSIBILITIES OF PERSONAL HOLINESS

Summarizing the Chapter

Being people of integrity means Christians will diligently cultivate a lifestyle of personal holiness in such matters as sexual purity, material contentment, doctrinal soundness, and sincerity of love.

Getting Started (Choose One)

1. We all encounter commercial messages in many forms each day. Tell about a recent one that you have heard frequently. Has it become tiresome yet for you? How does it promote discontentment?

2. What would be your number one choice for how contemporary society is most irresponsible (this can be a thought, philosophy, activity, neglect, etc.)? Has this affected your own behavior or apathy? If so, in what way and to what extent? In what practical ways can you avoid being affected like that?

Answering the Questions

1. What are three ways Christians can honor marriage?

2. What is covetousness, and how is it most frequently displayed, according to Scripture?

3. Name two of the four guidelines this chapter gives for attaining contentment and having scriptural support.

4. How does impure or poorly understood doctrine affect our Christian lives?

5. What are three specific false teachings that have harmed the church during its history?

6. What New Testament character trait is the centerpiece for all others?

7. What has constant exposure to contemporary, ungodly culture, its news and entertainment, done to most believers' sense of outrage?

8. What is the key to "cling[ing] to what is good" (Rom. 12:9)?

Focusing on Prayer

- Thank God for the possessions He has blessed you with and ask that He would grant you a greater degree of contentment.

- Sometime during the next week, devote special time to praying for your nation and community. Ask the Lord to make you and other believers more sensitive to evil and injustice and more determined to stand for what is right.

Applying the Truth

Choose a two-week time period in the near future in which you watch less television daily. Reduce the time by at least one hour per day, and plan for a substitute use of your time. Keep a written record of your progress, and jot down what God teaches you along the way. (If you have no television, schedule some extra reading time, either of Scripture or of a Christian book you have been meaning to read.)

CHAPTER 10:

THE OBLIGATIONS OF PRACTICAL HOLINESS

Summarizing the Chapter

When we are committed to the concept of personal holiness over the long term, that attitude will reflect itself in genuine love and practical concern and good works toward others—fellow believers and unbelievers.

Getting Started (Choose One)

1. What connotation does the term *obligation* have for you? Does it become less negative if you apply it toward family matters in contrast to job concerns? Why or why not?

2. In general, do you think people are more hardworking or more laid back than they were a generation ago? Give some reasons and examples to support your answer.

Answering the Questions

1. What is the most elemental demonstration we can give of brotherly love (see Phil. 2:3-4)?

2. What must we avoid when we are giving honor to other believers?

3. Hard work and the negative effects of laziness are like the two sides of a coin. What are these differing but detrimental results?

4. How does the Greek meaning of "fervent" in Romans 12:11 help us understand Paul's teaching here?

5. What two factors do we need to consider when we examine our priorities for serving Christ?

6. How does the biblical usage of *hope* differ from the way people commonly understand that term today (see Rom. 8:24-25)?

7. What is one of the principles the apostles were so devoted to that they were prompted to select deacons (Acts 6:3-4)?

8. How is the second part of Hebrews 13:2 often misunderstood? How should it actually be interpreted?

9. What practical, specific examples did Jesus give for how we are to treat those who mistreat us (Luke 6:29-30)?

10. List three of the five practical ways we can sympathize or empathize with others. What Scripture references support your list?

11. What is Paul warning against in the final phrase of Romans 12:16? Do other references in the Bible warn against the same thing?

12. What does Exodus 21:23-25 mean, and how does it apply to believers today?

13. What does it mean to "heap burning coals upon his head" (Rom. 12:20)? What Old Testament verses relate to this principle?

Focusing on Prayer

• Think about Francis Schaeffer's quote at the opening of this chapter. Ask the Lord to make you more of the kind of believer described there.

- Pray for someone at your workplace or school whom you have found difficult to get along with. Ask God to show you some practical way to love that person.

Applying the Truth

Memorize Romans 12:10-13, and ask a Christian friend or relative to keep you accountable as you learn it.

SCRIPTURE INDEX

5:25	96
5:30	96
6:37	144
7:30	96
8:31	34
9:4	141
10:27	22
11:35	151
13:3-17	164
13:14-17	41
13:20	120
13:35	133, 139
15:1-5	47
15:5	110
15:8	48
15:13	41
16:33	67
17:1	96
17:12	29
17:15-18	117
17:17-21	31

Acts

1:8	110
1:14	145
2:40	20
2:42	145
2:42, 44	146
4:32	146
5:1-11	29
6:3-4	145, 176
9	17
9:31	84
10:34	152
17:16-17	91
20:24	65, 166
20:28	120
20:29-30	30
21:10-12	65
21:10-14	166
23—26	61
24:14	33
26:22-24	88

Romans

1:1	143
1:5	96
1:9	143
1:13	47
1:13-16	91
2:11	152
3:1-2	31
3:20-24	108
3:24-26	89
5:3-5	145
5:5	40
5:6-8	89
6	21
6:4	24
6:8	89
6:19	109
7:4	39, 163
7:14-15, 19-22	134
7:14-25	50
7:18	93
7:24	111
8:24-25	144, 176
8:28	130
9:1-3; 10:1	92
12	76, 156
12:1	85
12:1-2	21, 75, 136
12:2	viii, 44
12:3	140
12:9	132, 133, 134, 136, 174
12:10	140
12:10-13	139, 177
12:11	141, 142, 143, 176
12:12	144, 145
12:13	146, 147
12:14	148, 154
12:14-16	148
12:15	150
12:16	151, 152, 153, 176
12:17	154, 155
12:17-21	154
12:18	156
12:19	156

2:8-9	108
2:10	47
3:20	24, 111
4:1	109
4:12-13	31
4:13	22
4:14	30
4:17-19	19
4:20	19
4:22	20
4:23-24	21
4:24	21
4:32	41
5:1-2	41
5:3, 5-6	127
5:8-10	44
5:9	47
5:15-16	141
5:15-17	44
6:18	145
6:19	123

Philippians

1:1	143
1:3-4	120
1:9	40, 41
1:9-11	40
1:10	42, 44, 45, 46
1:11	47, 48
1:16	34
1:20-21	89
1:27-28	61
2:3	140, 153
2:3-4	139, 175
2:12	108, 109, 171
2:12-13	105, 107, 171
2:13	110, 111, 112, 171
2:18	121
3:5-6	17
3:7-8	17
3:8	17, 22
3:9	23
3:10	24, 25

3:11	25
3:14	17
3:20	49
3:20-21	26
4:8	44, 136
4:14	150

Colossians

1:29	142, 143
3	21
3:1-17	109, 160
3:2	131
3:12	151
3:16	21, 34
4:18	150

1 Thessalonians

3:12	133
4:3-4	128
4:9	140
5	135
5:8	144
5:10	20
5:12-13	120
5:17	145
5:18	118
5:21	44
5:21-22	135
5:22	63
5:25	150

2 Thessalonians

1:11	150
3:1	150

1 Timothy

1:15	93
1:17	85
2:8	145

GENERAL INDEX

Edwards, Jonathan and Sarah, 49
Ephesus, 32
Epistle to the Philippians, The (F.B. Meyer), 23
Eve, 132
Ezra, 37

Fear of God, reverence, 84, 85, 109, 110, 134
Felix, 33
Festus, 88
First and Second Peter and First John (Alexander Maclaren), 48
Flying Scotsman, The (Sally Magnuson), 15
Forgotten Spurgeon, The (Iain Murray), 81, 82

Gospel, the, vii, viii, 20, 31, 35, 36, 61, 91, 92, 126, 132, 138
Grace, 20, 37, 50, 90, 140
Great Evangelical Disaster, The (Francis Schaeffer), 138

Hagar, 28
Hananiah, Mishael and Azariah see *Shadrach, Meshach, and Abed-nego*
Hannah, 131
Hiebert, D. Edmond, 38
Holiness, 21, 39, 41, 85, 123-124, 125 (Chapter 9 *passim*), 137 (Chapter 10 *passim*)
Hudson Taylor's Spiritual Secret (Howard and Geraldine Taylor), 69, 70
Humility, 94, 95, 97, 98, 99, 120, 140, 151, 155

Huntingdon, Lady, 49
Hypocrisy, ix, x, 18, 46, 83, 103 (Chapter 7 *passim*), 133, 139, 140

Integrity, see esp. ix, x, xi, 16, 22, 24, 26, 31, 32, 35, 37, 40, 41, 45, 51, 60, 76, 79, 83, 89, 91, 103, 109, 111, 112, 119, 123, 125, 128, 132, 134, 140, 147, 156, 158
Isaiah, 79
Ishmael, 28
Israel, nation of, ix, x, 28, 31

Jacob, 130
Job, 73, 79
John the Baptist. 61, 63
Joseph, 64
Judas, 29

Latimer, Hugh, 27
Lazarus, 151
Leadership in the church, ix, x, 30, 31, 36, 37, 83, 119, 120, 121, 122, 123, 147
submission to, 119, 120, 121
Lemuel, 63
Liddell, Eric, 15, 16
Liddell, Florence, 16
Lloyd-Jones, Martyn, 125
Love, 40, 41, 42, 120, 133, 134, 137, 138, 139, 140, 151
Luther, Martin, 27, 49

Maclaren, Alexander, 48
Magnuson, Sally, 15, 16
Martha, 115, 116, 151
Martyn, Henry, 142